# LifeJourney Books

## Do-It-Yourself Memoir Workbook

## Naomi Grossman
## Deborah Fineblum

Any reproduction of these materials is prohibited without the written consent of the authors.

Contact us at info@lifejourneybooks.com

ISBN: 0615675700
ISBN-13: 9780615675701

To my children Jonathan and Joselyn, Rebecca and Rafi and Leah and Gershon, and to their children, Bentzion Yair, Ayelet Rina, Nachum Tuvya Kalev, Amiel Adin, Asher Sivan and Shifra Chaya Raizel Adira. It is your generations who inspire us to rescue, record and share these LifeStories.

D.F.


To Tzvi, Yosef, Pnina, Aron, Naftali and Aliza –
Thank you doesn't seem sufficient but it's all I got. I love you.

N.G.


And in gratitude to all those who have shared their precious life stories with us in LifeJourney Books memoir-writing "Boot Camps" around the country and around the world. Your honesty and your courage have made this book possible.

# Table of Contents

# Table of Contents

# 1 Welcome to Your Life!

## An Introduction to Your *LifeJourney Books Do-It-Yourself Memoir Workbook*

*How would you have felt if, before she died, your grandmother had handed you the book of her life? It would have included the things that mattered to her in all their rich detail: from the hopscotch she played with her best friend to the birth of her baby brother in the middle of the night to the soldiers marching outside her window to the thrill of her first kiss.*

SADLY, YOU CAN'T BRING her back to tell you her story. But, what she wasn't able to do for you, you *can* do for your children, grandchildren and all your loved ones.

You've already begun the journey. Everything you need to tell your life story is in the book you hold in your hands, and we'll be with you every step of the way.

But before we begin, we have to erase four insidious thoughts that could stop you cold – and might even have derailed your memoir-writing efforts in the past:

- My life is not very interesting. It's no different from anyone else's.
- My family would never be interested in hearing my story.
- I'm not a good writer.
- I don't have the time to write.

OK, we've said them. Now let's take them on … one roadblock at a time.

### My life is not very interesting. It's no different from anyone else's.

No two lives are identical, even brothers and sisters or best friends who've lived through the same experiences will surprise you by remembering things completely differently. Your life story with its surprises, its laughter, its disappointments and its joys is as unique as your fingerprints – or your wrinkles – and you are the only one who has been there for the entire journey.

### My family would never be interested in hearing my story.

Just like your grandmother's life story is precious to you, yours will mean so much to your family. Grandchildren who are small now or teenage nieces caught up in their own lives will someday long to know what your life was all about. Know that you are part of a fascinating generation, one shaped by powerful historical

*"We write to heighten our own awareness of life. We write to taste life twice, in the moment and in retrospection. We write to be able to transcend our life, to reach beyond it… to teach ourselves to speak with others, to record the journey into the labyrinth."*

—ANAIS NIN

# Welcome...

and cultural influences – by war and hardship, by your own music, books, movies and even dance steps. And your descendants will be curious about where their daughter's musical talent comes from and their son's wacky sense of humor. Plus they'll want to know how and why you made the choices you did.

## I can't write.

Whether or not you were the top grammar student in your class, you are the perfect – and only – person to write this story. That's because there's nothing as intimate as our own lives and you are the only one who knows how it feels to be you. Just answer the questions honestly and don't get tripped up on punctuation, pronouns and past participles. Tell it in your own words and include the all-important details to make your story come alive. And we guarantee you'll surprise yourself by remembering more than you think you will.

## I don't have the time.

You're absolutely right: there are more things to get done than there are hours in the day. But, when you think about it, isn't setting the record straight about your life worth making the time for? Perhaps you can get a group of friends to do this project together or ask a relative or aide to help you answer these questions. Or maybe you and your spouse or your good friend can work on your *LifeJourney Books Do-It-Yourself Memoir Workbooks* at the kitchen table together.

But, whether you're working as a group, a pair or going solo, you're always better off setting aside a block of time each day to answer as many questions as you can. For night people, it can be after the dishes are done (your TV show can wait). For morning folks, it's great to get writing before the other daytime activities distract you. Before you know it, you'll find yourself rushing through your breakfast cereal to get back to your story.

But even the most dedicated life storyteller needs the occasional boost. Here are some powerful motivators you'll want to take with you on your LifeJourney. Be sure to return to this section any time your "writing batteries" need recharging.

## Life didn't just happen to you. You happened to life.

Sometimes we all feel like victims of fate or destiny but the truth is your life is not just a series of accidents – it's a strange and wonderful journey packed with patterns, priorities and principles. Your choices reveal everything about the

> *"We all come from the past and children ought to know what went into their making, to know that life is a braided cord of humanity stretching up from time long gone, and that it cannot be defined by the span of a single journey from diaper to shroud."*
> —RUSSELL BAKER

> *"You may, in the privacy of your heart take out the album of your own life and search it for the people and places you have loved and learned from …and for those moments in the past – any of them half forgotten – through which you glimpsed, however dimly and fleetingly, the sacredness of your own journey."*
> —FREDERICK BUECHNER

values you hold dear. This is something you will be able to see clearly only after you complete your *LifeJourney Books Do-It-Yourself Memoir Workbook*.

### You are still the same person you were at 8.

Many of your responses as an adult could have been predicted by closely observing your childhood self. The you who wouldn't let another child be pushed around by the playground bully is the same you who won't allow their friend be taken advantage of now by an unscrupulous scam artist. You will begin to see how you have grown and developed but also who you are – and have always been – at your deepest core.

### Wrestling with the Past.

Sadly, even the happiest of lives have their share of sorrow. We have seen with our students how much courage it can take to face some of our most painful memories. But this encounter with life's difficult moments also gives us perspective. We predict that, by the time you've completed your *LifeJourney Books Do-It-Yourself Memoir Workbook*, you'll better understand – and possibly be able to forgive or come to terms with – those who may have hurt you, as you make peace with the past and even find yourself

able at long last to lay some of your personal demons to rest.

### The kids need to hear it.

Retracing your steps transmits the precious legacy of your life and values to children, grandchildren, nieces, nephews and generations yet unborn, all living in very different times than you have. Remember that by sharing your life experiences, you also share your wisdom, gained from the many hard-won lessons you've learned along the way. And, because you are so much a part of your family, your life story has the power to inspire them and inform the way they – and their children after them – live their lives.

### Families come in all shapes and sizes.

No two families are alike, so if a certain question or chapter does not pertain to you, feel free to change the wording of the question to suit your experience. Never married? See Chapter 14 for your chance to share the friendships that enrich your life. No kids? Tell us about your favorite nieces, nephews, godchildren, your beloved students or the little boy next door who in so many ways grew to be part of your family. If a chapter or a question really doesn't apply, even with your liberal editing, feel free to skip over it and we'll meet up with you in the next chapter!

# Welcome...

**Remember that life is in the details. So be generous with them.**

Each time you add a telling detail – the braying laugh of your favorite radio soap opera character, the sight of a train carrying a loved-one off to war, the smell of popcorn and cotton candy on the boardwalk of your honeymoon – you transport yourself and your reader back to the time and place you're remembering.

**You're doing it for them, but you'll be amazed at what YOU gain.**

Chances are the main reason you're telling your life story now is for your children, grandchildren and future generations. But in the process of giving them this gift, something magical happens: You receive an even greater gift. As you share your experiences with your loved ones, you begin to understand your life and truly see who you are. Your philosophy of life, your guiding principles, your strengths and yes, even your weaknesses reveal themselves. As the whole picture begins to emerge, you'll begin at long last to recognize those values at your deepest core and see how they have guided your footsteps every step of the way.

**Instructions for using your LifeJourney Books Do-It-Yourself Memoir Workbook**

We have provided extra pages at the end of each chapter for you to respond to Today's Tips or to be used for overflow for your answers to the chapter questions. Please never allow space limitations to limit your memory flow. Hint: The more you are able to fill up the lines and extra pages provided, the richer and more complete your memoir will be.

**A word to the novice memoirist:**

Don't worry that you can't remember exactly how it all happened – and don't let anybody tell you that your memories are inaccurate or don't reflect the way it really was. If they do, you have our permission to tell them they're welcome to pick up their own copy of *LifeJourney Books Do-It-Yourself Memoir Workbook* and write it the way they remember it. But this is your chance to tell it the way you experienced it.

Sure, your kids and grandkids, your husband or wife, brothers and sisters and even your friends know different parts of you.

But who's the one who knows your whole story?

Only you.

**... So let's get started!**

*"One may merely know that no one is alone and hope that a singular story, as every true story is singular, will in the magic way of some things apply, connect, resonate, touch a major chord."*
—GEOFFREY WOLFF

## 2 Pivotal Life Events Timeline (PLET)

You are now ready to embark upon the telling of your Life Story. Please turn the page to start your **Pivotal Life Events Timeline (PLET)**. Be sure to return to your PLET each time you complete a chapter and have recalled more Pivotal Events to add.

# PLET
## Pivotal Life Events Timeline

Please add the date and pivotal life event as we have here—and then continue to fill in the dates and events on the lines provided after you complete each chapter. *Note:* You will want to include every event that was destined to change your life, from the obvious milestones to seemingly minor experiences that would have a big impact down the road.

**June 14, 1939**

Grandma gives me

a violin for my

9th Birthday

I am born

Remember to Return Here After Each Chapter to Add Those Pivotal Life Events

Remember to Return Here After Each Chapter to Add Those Pivotal Life Events

Feel free to use these extra pages to share more pivotal memories and stories!

**1. Where are you?** Your grandmother's kitchen? Your uncle's boat? Your family's backyard? Is it a familiar scene to you or a special journey you were on, an adventure that took you out of your regular setting?

_____

_____

_____

_____

_____

_____

_____

**2. What are you doing?** Perhaps it's a moment of intense change or trauma; your family had to flee their home and you're clutching your rag doll to your chest. Or it may be an average day; you're sitting in your high chair eating blueberries and watching your mother wash dishes.

_____

_____

_____

_____

_____

_____

_____

IN THIS FREE-WRITING activity, designed to call forth your first conscious memory, you will begin the process of warming up and flexing your writer "muscles." No special skill or talent is required – as you allow the exercise to fling open the door to a stream of long-forgotten images, recollections and feelings that will make up the core of your LifeJourney process.

That's why the spirit of adventure and creativity, the honesty (especially when it's hard) and the patience you bring to this exercise will build a strong foundation for our work together. The good news: This attitude will pay off not only in what you are able to remember today but in everything about your one-of-a-kind life story that you will be invited to bring to the LifeJourney process in upcoming chapters.

Because the secret to recapturing that far distant time lies in both the honest telling and the remembering and sharing of details (the combined smell of coffee and wood chips in your father's workroom), once you read these instructions over once and then a second time, we're going to ask you to close your eyes and travel back with us over the years to your first conscious memory.

Go way back, far back in time, well before you think you can remember - even if it's just a glimpse or snippet of a memory. Don't judge the memory or chase it, just be patient with yourself and when something does surface, welcome it like an old friend.

*As you recall and begin* to jot down these important clues to your earliest memory, don't worry about grammar or spelling or punctuation – or even strict accuracy about the details of the moment we are asking you to recreate. Fussing over these little things can stop cold the flow of memories you need to recall the most formative times of your life. So just let yourself relax back in time and, taking your time, record what you remember exactly as you remember it.

3. **How old are you?** Alas, there is probably no calendar on the wall telling you the date. But, if you know when your sister was born and she's an infant in this memory or if your mother is pregnant, that could help. Or you can base the timing on where you're living or if a certain relative is still alive at this moment in time. Or if there's a war on and your uncle is going off to serve. Sometimes seeing how big your hands look or the clothing you're wearing can also help date a memory.

_____

_____

_____

_____

_____

4. **Whom do you see around you?** What family members, friends or schoolmates are in this scene? Can you describe them and what they're doing?

_____

_____

_____

_____

_____

_____

**Just remembered something else?**
**Use your extra pages at the end of this chapter!**

5. **What do you hear, smell and taste?** Interestingly, scientists are finding that the sense of smell has a particular power to evoke previously forgotten moments in time. Tastes too can be unforgettable and maybe at that moment you are enjoying a special childhood treat. In addition, we can all testify that the music we grew up with can also take us back over the decades in unexpected and wonderful ways.

_____

_____

_____

_____

_____

_____

_____

6. **How and what did you feel at that minute?** Were you happy? Excited? Afraid? Once you have a good idea of what you were feeling at the time, you can then ask yourself: Are there are any clues in the scene to help me understand *why* you felt this way? Was your father going off to war? Your big sister getting married? The dog next door growling menacingly at you from behind the fence?

_____

_____

_____

_____

_____

**7.** As an adult looking back on this memory, what insights into your youngest self, your family and that time of history does this memory evoke?

_____

_____

_____

_____

_____

_____

_____

_____

_____

_____

_____

_____

_____

_____

_____

_____

_____

**Don't Forget to PLET!**

Now that you've finished Chapter 3, please return to your Pivotal Life Event Timeline (PLET) on pages 6-9 to fill in more key events and dates. You'll be glad you did!!

# Feel Free to use these extra pages to share more memories and stories.

LIFEJOURNEY
BOOKS

# 4 Me: The Early Years, Birth to 5

1. **Why did your parents give you the name they did?** Are you named after someone? If so, whom? What do you know about him/her? Or did they just like the name? (Was it popular at the time and, if so, why?)

_____

_____

_____

_____

_____

_____

_____

_____

_____

_____

_____

_____

_____

_____

_____

_____

_____

_____

_____

ET'S START AT the very beginning, when you made your grand entrance into the world. You might need help with some of these memories – only an older sibling can tell you how you kept everyone up at night with your crying and when you bestowed your first smile on your family. But as you begin to recall your early childhood you'll delight in remembering so many "firsts" - your first doll or toy train, your first friend, your first babysitter. This was an age when you began to discover the wonders of the world. And we hope you enjoy returning to that magical time.

Dig out the old photo albums and spread pictures of yourself as a baby and young child around the table. If you can, include photos of your parents and siblings from that era to help jog your memory.

## Quick Quote

"Where you end up is not the most important thing. It's the road you take to get there. The road you take is what you'll look back on and call your life."

— TIM WILEY

## Life-Bit

"I was a much longed-for baby. It wasn't for want of trying that my parents were childless for so long."

— MADELEINE L'ENGLE, *The Summer of the Great-grandmother*

2. **What were you like as a baby?** Do you recall your parents or siblings discussing your early temperament? Did you cry a lot? Or were you an easy, placid baby? (Bonus question: How does your adult personality reflect your temperament as a baby?)

_____

_____

_____

_____

_____

_____

_____

_____

_____

_____

_____

_____

_____

_____

_____

_____

_____

3. **If you have older siblings, were they excited or jealous by your appearance in the household?** If you can, call them and ask them how they felt about your arrival. If you can't, what might they have said?

_____

_____

_____

_____

_____

_____

_____

_____

_____

_____

_____

_____

_____

_____

_____

_____

_____

_____

_____

Did your father have a nickname? Your mother? Your siblings? Write down all the nicknames in your family and, if you can, the reasons for them.

## Quick Quote

"Nicknames stick to people, and the most ridiculous are the most adhesive."

— THOMAS C. HALIBURTON

## Life-Bit

"One day I was approached by one of the editors and asked if I'd like to write a monthly column about the children in H. That was when at the age of nine, my love of writing actually began. I called my column "Small Fry," a nickname Peter had given me."

— GLORIA PARIS,
*A Child of Sanitariums:
A Memoir of
Tuberculosis Survival
and Lifelong Disability*

4. **Did you have a special nickname?** Why were you called that? Did it stick? How did you feel about it?

_____

_____

_____

_____

_____

_____

_____

_____

_____

_____

_____

_____

_____

_____

_____

_____

_____

_____

**Note: Feel free to answer all Today's Tips and overflow from Questions on the extra pages after each chapter.**

## 5. What were your favorite toys? Did you love building with blocks? Playing with dolls? Chasing balls? Riding on the seesaw? Try to remember a specific experience with one of your playthings.

_____

_____

_____

_____

_____

_____

_____

_____

_____

_____

_____

_____

_____

_____

_____

_____

_____

Draw your special doll or your security blanket, your favorite stuffed animal or whatever helped get you through childhood.

## Quick Quote

"It's not so much that we're afraid of change or so in love with the old ways, but it's that place in between that we fear … It's like being between trapezes. It's Linus when his blanket is in the dryer. There's nothing to hold on to."

— MARILYN FERGUSON

## Life-Bit

"I had no brother or sisters, my parents could hardly afford to buy me any toys or games, and television and computers had not yet been born."

— AMOS OZ,
*A Tale of Love and Darkness*

6. **Did you have a security blanket?** A special doll? A stuffed animal that never left your side? Please describe whatever it was as accurately as you can. Can you remember how it made you feel?

_____

_____

_____

_____

_____

_____

_____

_____

_____

_____

_____

_____

_____

_____

_____

_____

_____

_____

_____

**7.** **Do you recall any special lullabies?** Please record the lyrics as best you can. Do you remember how you felt when you heard it as a child?

_____

_____

_____

_____

_____

_____

_____

_____

_____

_____

_____

_____

_____

_____

_____

_____

_____

_____

_____

_____

_____

If you can, try to find out what happened to your first friend.

"Little friends may prove great friends."

— AESOP

"Lesson One: Being a starlet is a complicated life, especially when you are four years old."

— SHIRLEY TEMPLE, *Child Star: An Autobiography*

8. **Who was your first friend?** Can you remember his or her name? What did you play? Why was he or she your friend? (Were your parents friends or relatives?)

_____

_____

_____

_____

_____

_____

_____

_____

_____

_____

_____

_____

_____

_____

_____

_____

_____

**Just remembered something else?**
**Feel free to use your extra pages at the end of this chapter.**

## 9. What were your mother's and father's parenting styles?

Who was the disciplinarian? Who gave in when you cried? Who did you call for at night when you woke up with a bad dream or tummy ache? If possible, ask your siblings to corroborate – or refute – what you remember.

_____

_____

_____

_____

_____

_____

_____

_____

_____

_____

_____

_____

_____

_____

_____

_____

_____

If you can, ask your children if they see similarities between you and any memories they may have of your parents, their Grandma and Grandpa.

## Quick Quote

"No two siblings have the same parents."

— GENIE ZEIGLER

## Life-Bit

"My father had an Irish quickness both to anger and to mirth…he was a strict and stern disciplinarian and I tried to follow my mother's example of not crossing him when he was in a bad mood."

— RICHARD NIXON, _The Memoirs of Richard Nixon_

## Quick Quote

"My parents used to take me to the pet department and tell me it was a zoo."

— BILLY CONNOLLY

## Life-Bit

"I remember the sail, the sunset and the lighthouse pictured on that pail but I cannot recall the dog's name and this bothers me."

— VLADIMIR NABAKOV, *Speak, Memory*

**10.** **Did your family have a pet?** A dog? A cat? A gerbil? Can you remember what your relationship with the pet was?

_____

_____

_____

_____

_____

_____

_____

_____

_____

_____

_____

_____

_____

_____

_____

_____

_____

**11.** **What is your first memory of school?** What grade did you start in? Do you remember your first day? Share any memories you have of your first school experiences.

_____

_____

_____

_____

_____

_____

_____

_____

_____

_____

_____

_____

_____

_____

_____

_____

_____

_____

_____

_____

Do a Google map search for your first school (or have someone help you).

## Quick Quote

"A child educated only at school is an uneducated child."

— GEORGE SATAYANA

## Life-Bit

"Preschool was fun for me. I got to be around kids for a change. Being an only child, I longed for a playmate."

— MEILENA HAUSLENDALE, _Onward Rising: A Memoir_

## Quick Quote

"The reason grandchildren and grandparents get along so well is that they have a common enemy."

— SAM LEVENSON

## Life-Bit

"I can still roam that landscape of my childhood and again experience lights, smells, people, rooms, moments, gestures, tones of voice and objects."

— INGMAR BERGMAN, *The Magic Lantern*

**12.** **Who took care of you most in your toddler years?** Your mother? Your grandmother? A sibling? A nanny? Describe how you felt about this early relationship.

_____

_____

_____

_____

_____

_____

_____

_____

_____

_____

_____

_____

_____

_____

_____

_____

_____

### Don't forget to PLET!

**Now return to Chapter 2 to add Pivotal Life Events you remembered during this chapter. You'll be glad you did!!**

# Off to School: The Elementary Era

**5**

1. **Where did you live?** What was it like to grow up on your street and in your home? Please give us an example of a typical evening in your neighborhood.

IS THERE ANY PHASE in life more filled with hope, awe and wonder than those early years at school? At this age, nearly everything feels fresh and exciting - from strolling with your best friend to the corner store for penny candy to losing your first tooth to playing ball in the street for hours until your mother calls you "for the last time" to come in for supper. These are the memories that begin to define the adult you would become.

Gather family photos and official papers and documents from your school years, even old library cards and letters. Keep them handy as you work through the exercises. You'll be surprised at the memories they bring back!

## Quick Quote

"All of us have moments in our childhood where we come alive for the first time. And we go back to those moments and think, this is when I became myself."

— RITA DOVE

## Life-Bit

"… my memories are of friction between my father and mother. They seemed to be nearly always at odds…. An educated woman, I suppose, can't resist the temptation to correct an uneducated man."

— MALCOLM X,
*The Autobiography of Malcolm X*

2. **Where were you in the family birth order?** How did you get along with each of your siblings at this age? Please describe. If there were favorite children in your family, were you either parent's favorite? If not, who was?

_____

_____

_____

_____

_____

_____

_____

_____

_____

_____

_____

_____

_____

_____

_____

_____

_____

_____

_____

_____

_____

_____

## 3. Describe a typical morning in your house. Include as many details as you can!

_____

_____

_____

_____

_____

_____

_____

_____

_____

_____

_____

_____

_____

_____

_____

_____

_____

_____

_____

_____

_____

_____

_____

Jot down five words to describe each parent and sibling living at home during this stage of your childhood. Hint: Don't think too long about it. The first answers to come to mind are almost always the truest.

## Quick Quote

"Love at first sight is easy to understand; it's when two people have been looking at each other for a lifetime that it becomes a miracle."

— AMY BLOOM

## Life-Bit

"Such a house, oh such a house it was … It was that wonderful 'home of our own' that my mother had dreamed about all those Depression years."

— RUSSELL BAKER,
*The Good Times*

4. **What did you learn about marriage from your parents?**
Did they seem happy? How did they relate to each other?
Please describe a "typical" interchange between your
mother and father.

_____

_____

_____

_____

_____

_____

_____

_____

_____

_____

_____

_____

_____

_____

_____

_____

_____

_____

5. **What was a favorite activity with each parent from this era?** Please describe these activities and how you felt.

_____

_____

_____

_____

_____

_____

_____

_____

_____

_____

_____

_____

_____

_____

_____

_____

_____

_____

_____

_____

_____

**Quick Quote**

"What children need most are the essentials that grandparents provide in abundance. They give unconditional love, kindness, patience, humor, comfort, lessons in life. And, most importantly, cookies."

— RUDOLPH GIULIANI

**Life-Bit**

"Grandmother told me about the World, about Life but also about Death (which was occupying my thoughts a good deal at the time) … She listened carefully, saw through my fibs or brushed them aside with friendly irony. She allowed me to have my say as a real person in my own right without camouflage."

— INGMAR BERGMAN, *The Magic Lantern: An Autobiography*

6. **Can you describe a grandparent or other loving older person in your childhood?** Can you tell us about a particularly happy memory with them?

_____

_____

_____

_____

_____

_____

_____

_____

_____

_____

_____

_____

_____

_____

_____

_____

_____

_____

_____

## 7. Who were your best friends or playmates at the time?

What did you do together? If you can, please describe some memorable moments with these friends.

_____

_____

_____

_____

_____

_____

_____

_____

_____

_____

_____

_____

_____

_____

_____

_____

_____

_____

_____

Name one historical moment that greatly impacted your childhood. Please write on your extra page a possible newspaper "headline" signifying that moment.

## Quick Quote

"History does not repeat itself. The historians repeat one another."

— MAX BEERBOHM

## Life-Bit

"Lately I have developed a great love for family trees … and have come to the conclusion that, once you begin, you want to delve still deeper into the past, and you can keep on making fresh and interesting discoveries."

— ANNE FRANK, *Diary of A Young Girl*

8. **What were the historical events taking place during your childhood and how were you aware of them?**

_____

_____

_____

_____

_____

_____

_____

_____

_____

_____

_____

_____

_____

_____

_____

_____

_____

**Just remembered something else?**
**Feel free to use your extra pages at the end of this chapter.**

## 9. Do you have a sad or scary memory from these years?

How did you feel? How did you respond to that challenge? How do you think it changed you?

_____

_____

_____

_____

_____

_____

_____

_____

_____

_____

_____

_____

_____

_____

_____

_____

_____

_____

_____

_____

_____

"If at first the idea is not absurd, then there is no hope for it."

— ALBERT EINSTEIN

"The sirloin steak was thirty-five cents a pound and the butcher would deliver. Butter was fifteen cents and nobody had ever heard of cholesterol."

— BOB HOPE,
*Don't Shoot, It's Only Me*

**10.** **Do you recall a favorite book, comic, movie or radio program from your childhood?** Can you describe your experience with them? How did they influence your ideas of the world and hopes for your future?

_____

_____

_____

_____

_____

_____

_____

_____

_____

_____

_____

_____

_____

_____

_____

_____

_____

_____

_____

## 11. Can you describe your first clear memory of school?

What did you enjoy most about school then? What was your favorite subject in elementary school? Tell us why and how it informed your future (or not).

_____

_____

_____

_____

_____

_____

_____

_____

_____

_____

_____

_____

_____

_____

_____

_____

_____

_____

_____

_____

## Quick Quote

"I've never let my school interfere with my education."

— MARK TWAIN

## Life-Bit

"At thirteen, as was the custom in our world, I was dispatched to school in Switzerland. Run by a certain Madame Subilia, the school's population consisted of a number of haughtily aristocratic English girls who found my wild Hungarian ways highly amusing until I won them over by writing naughty rhymes about our hated English teacher."

— ZSA ZSA GABOR,
*One Lifetime is Not Enough*

**12.** **Who was your most influential teacher during those early years?** Please describe her (or him) in as much detail as possible. What did you learn from that teacher, lessons you took with you into adulthood?

_____

_____

_____

_____

_____

_____

_____

_____

_____

_____

_____

_____

_____

_____

_____

_____

_____

## Don't forget to PLET!

**Now return to Chapter 2 to add Pivotal Life Events you remembered during this chapter. You'll be glad you did!!**

LIFEJOURNEY
BOOKS

# 6 Growing Up: My Teenage Years

**1.** **When was the first time you realized you weren't a kid anymore?** Tell us about that moment in your adolescence, with as many details as you can recall.

_____

_____

_____

_____

_____

_____

_____

_____

THERE ARE NO more intense - or memorable - times than those magical and crazy teen years. Here we explore the high school experience, confidantes and confidence-builders (and destroyers), the facts of life and first loves, all set against the backdrop of hometown life and world events.

_____

_____

_____

_____

_____

_____

_____

_____

_____

_____

_____

Do you have your high school yearbook? If so, flip through the pages until you find a picture of yourself and write a short description of the person you were (being both honest and kind). Note: No yearbook? Then any photo of you as a teen will do.

## Quick Quote

"You don't have to suffer to be a poet. Adolescence is enough suffering for anyone."

— JOHN CIARDI

## Life-Bit

"I have made a plan for my life, as I am in my teens, and no more a child. I am old for my age, and I don't care much for girl's things. People think I'm wild and queer but Mother understands and helps me."

— LOUISA MAY ALCOTT,
*The Journals of
Louisa May Alcott*

2. **How did you feel about the prospect of growing up: Excited?** Impatient? Frightened? Please describe. How did you view yourself then? And how did you expect you would change?

_____

_____

_____

_____

_____

_____

_____

_____

_____

_____

_____

_____

_____

_____

_____

_____

_____

**3.** **How did your relationship with your mother change during your teen years?** With your father? Please give examples.

_____

_____

_____

_____

_____

_____

_____

_____

_____

_____

_____

_____

_____

_____

_____

_____

_____

_____

_____

_____

_____

_____

## Today's Tip

List five words that describe each of your parents as you saw them in your teen years.

## Quick Quote

"To an adolescent, there is nothing in the world more embarrassing than a parent."

— DAVE BARRY

## Life-Bit

"Mother's head snapped up. 'You can't talk to me like that,' she said. 'I'm your mother.' 'If you want to be treated like a mother,' I said, 'you should act like one.'"

— JEANNETTE WALLS,
*The Glass Castle*

www.LifeJourneyBooks.com

## Quick Quote

"Our siblings push buttons that cast us in roles we felt sure we had let go of long ago – the baby, the peacekeeper, the caretaker, the avoider ... It doesn't seem to matter how much time has elapsed or how far we've traveled."

— JANE MERSKY LEDER

## Life-Bit

"I remember well how my mother asked me why I couldn't be a nice boy like (my brother) Wilfred; but I would think to myself that Wilfred, for being so nice and quiet, often stayed hungry. So early in life, I learned that, if you want something, you had better make some noise."

— MALCOLM X,
*The Autobiography of Malcolm X*

**4.** **How did your relationships with your siblings change during your teen years?** Please give examples to illustrate those changes.

## 5. Whom did you trust completely during those years? How was that relationship helpful to your becoming the person you are today?

_____

_____

_____

_____

_____

_____

_____

_____

_____

_____

_____

_____

_____

_____

_____

_____

_____

_____

_____

_____

### Today's Tip

What was your favorite book as a teen? Was there a character who modeled the kind of adult you hoped to be? Please share your impressions and the impact it had on you.

### Quick Quote

"A true friend is someone who thinks that you are a good egg even though he knows that you are slightly cracked."

— BERNARD MELTZER

### Life-Bit

"In 1920, I was twelve years old. Taller than most sixteen-year-olds in my neighborhood, I was 90 percent knees, elbows and other assorted bony parts."

— MILTON BERLE, *Milton Berle: An Autobiography*

## Quick Quote

"The mediocre teacher tells. The good teacher explains. The superior teacher demonstrates. The great teacher inspires."

— WILLIAM A. WARD

## Life-Bit

"The dream begins, most of the time, with a teacher who believes in you, who tugs and pushes, and leads you onto the next plateau, sometimes poking you with a sharp stick called truth."

— DAN RATHER,
*Rather Outspoken:
My Life in the News*

6. **Who was your favorite teacher in high school?** What did you learn from him or her?

_____

_____

_____

_____

_____

_____

_____

_____

_____

_____

_____

_____

_____

_____

_____

_____

_____

_____

_____

_____

*7.* **Who was your best friend in these years?** When you think of all the things you did together, which memories stand out?

_____

_____

_____

_____

_____

_____

_____

_____

_____

_____

_____

_____

_____

_____

_____

_____

_____

_____

_____

_____

## Quick Quote

"Don't laugh at a youth for his affectations; he is only trying on one face after another to find a face of his own."

— LOGAN PEARSALL SMITH

## Life-Bit

"It's really a wonder I haven't dropped all my ideals, because they seem so absurd and impossible to carry out. Yet I keep them because in spite of everything, I still believe that people are really good at heart."

— ANNE FRANK, *The Diary of Anne Frank*

**8.** **What were your dreams?** What did you think you were going to be when you grew up? How did those dreams turn out?

_____

_____

_____

_____

_____

_____

_____

_____

_____

_____

_____

_____

_____

_____

_____

_____

_____

_____

**Just remembered something else?**
**Feel free to use your extra pages at the end of this chapter.**

## 9. Who was your first love?

What are your fondest memories of that earliest romance? What did you learn from it? Looking back, are you glad or sad about how it turned out? Why?

_____

_____

_____

_____

_____

_____

_____

_____

_____

_____

_____

_____

_____

_____

_____

_____

_____

_____

_____

Try sketching the layout of your high school on the extra page. See if you can still identify the location of a memorable classroom and record the name of the teacher and subject he or she taught.

## Quick Quote

"There is nothing like returning to a place that remains unchanged to find the ways in which you yourself have altered."

— NELSON MANDELA

## Life-Bit

"I have always been somewhat precocious, both physically and mentally. So it seems that from a hereditary point of view, nature was very kind to me."

— MARTIN LUTHER KING, JR., *The Autobiography of Martin Luther King, Jr.*

**10.** **How would you describe your high school?** What memories of the place stand out most clearly to you now?

_____

_____

_____

_____

_____

_____

_____

_____

_____

_____

_____

_____

_____

_____

_____

_____

_____

_____

**11.** **Were you a good student in high school?** What was your strongest subject? Your weakest one? How did those early success and disappointments affect - and possibly predict - your life path? Please give an example.

_____

_____

_____

_____

_____

_____

_____

_____

_____

_____

_____

_____

_____

_____

_____

_____

_____

12. **What was the best thing about being a teenager at that point in history?** The worst thing? How did the events of the day color your worldview? Please give an example.

_____

_____

_____

_____

_____

_____

_____

_____

_____

_____

_____

_____

_____

_____

_____

### Don't forget to PLET!

Now return to Chapter 2 to add Pivotal Life Events you remembered during this chapter. You'll be glad you did!!

# On My Own: Becoming an Adult

**1. What were your options for your post-high school life?**
What path did you choose? Why did you make the choice(s) that you did?

_____

_____

_____

_____

_____

_____

_____

_____

_____

_____

_____

_____

_____

_____

_____

_____

_____

_____

_____

_____

WHETHER YOU WENT to college, the military or straight to work, you had your own unique way of tumbling out of your childhood nest. Your choices might have been born of necessity but they were yours and you'll want to remember why you made them. This was a time when life still seemed endless and dating became a more serious endeavor. Back then you were busy discovering who you were going to be and exploring how you were going to get there.

Do you still have your college transcript or military records? Mementos from your first job? Gather up any artifacts you can find from your post-high school life and keep them around as you work on this chapter.

## Quick Quote

"My mother said I must always be intolerant of ignorance but understanding of illiteracy. That some people, unable to go to school, were more educated and more intelligent than college professors."

— MAYA ANGELOU

## Life-Bit

"I loathed every day and regret every day I spent in school. I like to be taught to read and write and add and then be left alone. I regret all the time I spent in public school. It was a blessing to be thrown out of college."

— WOODY ALLEN,
ROBERT E. KAPSIS,
KATHIE COBLENTZ,
*Woody Allen: Interviews*

2. **Did you go to college?** Why or why not? Please tell us about that time of your life in some detail.

**3.** **Did most of your friends go to college?** Or straight to work or to the Army? Why did they make these choices? Please share one of their experiences.

_____

_____

_____

_____

_____

_____

_____

_____

_____

_____

_____

_____

_____

_____

_____

_____

_____

_____

_____

_____

## Today's Tip

Can you remember the name of your first boss? Please describe what he or she was like.

## Quick Quote

"It is the working man who is the happy man. It is the idle man who is the miserable man."

— BENJAMIN FRANKLIN

## Life-Bit

"The same year the very coach that once had coached me in football relieved me of my job of junior varsity basketball coach because he felt I favored the "coloreds." As a senior I had surmised that this coach had a brain the size and density of a Ping-Pong ball so it came as no great surprise when he banished me forever from his gymnasium. But I was tired of fighting."

— PAT CONROY,
*The Water is Wide*

www.LifeJourneyBooks.com

Like or unlike you, did your own children live at home after high school or college? If so, what was it like for you? Ask them what the experience was like for them and prepare yourself for an honest answer!

## Quick Quote

"Children are our second chance to have a great parent-child relationship."

— LAURA SCHLESSINGER

## Life-Bit

"We felt that our parents were the best two people in the world – that we were wildly lucky to be their children. And we still feel that way."

— KATHERINE HEPBURN, *Me: Stories of My Life*

4. **As an older teen, were you living at home?** At school? On your own? Describe your relationship with your parents at this point.

**5.** **As an older teen, were you involved in your siblings' lives?** Did you have much interaction with them? Did they have an impact on your life at this point? Please describe your relationship(s).

_____

_____

_____

_____

_____

_____

_____

_____

_____

_____

_____

_____

_____

_____

_____

_____

_____

## Today's Tip

Call up your siblings if you can and ask them what their impressions were of you as a teen. If you can't call them, try to imagine how they would have answered this question and answer as if you were each of them.

## Quick Quote

"Sometimes being a brother is even better than being a superhero."

— MARC BROWN

## Life-Bit

"Rosetta was the eldest sister and the smartest of all my siblings. From her perch atop her bed – a bed, incidentally, that she shared with no one – Rosetta sat regally on a throne of bed pillows, legs crossed Buddha fashion, while drinking ice water, listening to her favorite public radio station, WBAI, and giving commands all day."

— JAMES MCBRIDE,
_The Color Of Water:
A Black Man's Tribute
To His White Mother_

6. **What were the significant historical events at this time?** How did they impact your choices? (For instance, did you or a loved one enlist? Or were you or he drafted?) Please tell us about that time.

_____

_____

_____

_____

_____

_____

_____

_____

_____

_____

_____

_____

_____

_____

_____

_____

_____

_____

_____

## 7. Were you thinking about a career at this point in your life?

What was it? Who or what was your primary motivating force behind that choice? (A parent? A grandparent? A teacher?) Looking back on it, was that a good thing? Why or why not?

_____

_____

_____

_____

_____

_____

_____

_____

_____

_____

_____

_____

_____

_____

_____

_____

_____

_____

_____

_____

Please write the best piece of advice you received from your mother or father in these formative years and the date as closely as you can recall.

### Quick Quote

"Parents can only give good advice or put them on the right paths, but the final forming of a person's character lies in their own hands."

— ANNE FRANK

### Life-Bit

"I am sometimes suspected of being nonreligious as an act of rebellion against Orthodox parents. That may have been true of my father but it was not true of me. I have rebelled against nothing. I have been left free and I have loved the freedom. The same is true of my brother and sister and our children."

— ISAAC ASIMOV,
*I, Asimov: A Memoir*

**8.** **When did you hear a parent's voice in your head?** Whose was it and what did it tell you? Did you listen? Why or why not?

_____

_____

_____

_____

_____

_____

_____

_____

_____

_____

_____

_____

_____

_____

_____

_____

_____

**Just remembered something else?**
**Use your extra pages at the end of this chapter.**

**9. Did you take dating seriously?** Were you involved with anyone? Did you feel like he or she was the love of your life? Describe the most significant romantic relationship you had in the post-high school years.

## Today's Tip

Can you remember the best date you had? What made it so memorable?

## Quick Quote

"When you're in a relationship and it's good, even if nothing else in your life is right, you feel like your whole world is complete."

— KEITH SWEAT

## Life-Bit

"I wasn't a cheerleader or a dancer and nobody ever asked me to the drive-in. I yearned for romance and dreamed of candlelight suppers, but I didn't have the nerve to invite Tommy Calfano to dinner."

— RUTH REICHL,
*Tender at the Bone: Growing up at the Table*

www.LifeJourneyBooks.com

Jot down a brief description of your best nights out during this time of your life. Don't skimp on the details!

## Quick Quote

"Life is partly what we make it, and partly what it is made by the friends we choose."

— TENNESSEE WILLIAMS

## Life-Bit

"In high school I got voted most likely to get voted for something. Even though I was the only one who voted, it still felt terrific being nominated."

— JAROD KINTZ

**10.** **As a young adult, did you stay connected to your high school friends?** Did you make new friends? What did you do for fun? To relax? Who did you spend time with? What kinds of activities did you do together?

## 11. Who was your primary influence in this period? How do you think that impacted the person you became?

_____

_____

_____

_____

_____

_____

_____

_____

_____

_____

_____

_____

_____

_____

_____

_____

_____

_____

_____

_____

_____

_____

_____

_____

_____

## Today's Tip

What words of wisdom would you tell someone who is just starting out in their career?

## Quick Quote

"Clothes make the man. Naked people have little or no influence on society."

— MARK TWAIN

## Life-Bit

"My teacher is so near to me that I scarcely think of myself apart from her. How much of my delight in all beautiful things is innate, and how much is due to her influence, I can never tell. I feel that her being is inseparable from my own, and that the footsteps of my life are in hers."

— HELEN KELLER,
ANNIE SULLIVAN,
_The Story of My Life_

Please describe the transition from being a student to being a worker.

"One's real life is often the life that one does not lead."

— OSCAR WILDE

"When I walk in and place my books on the teacher's desk they'll surely stop throwing things. But they don't. They ignore me and I don't know what to do till the words come out of my mouth, the first words I ever utter as a teacher, Stop throwing sandwiches. They look at me as if to say, 'Who's this guy?'"

— FRANK MCCOURT,
*Tis: A Memoir*

www.LifeJourneyBooks.com

## 12. Were you prepared to enter the world at this age?

If you had to do it over again, what would you have done differently? Why?

_____

_____

_____

_____

_____

_____

_____

_____

_____

_____

_____

_____

_____

_____

_____

_____

### Don't Forget to PLET!

**Now return to Chapter 2 to add Pivotal Life Events you remembered during this chapter. You'll be glad you did!!**

# Finding the Right One: The Courtship that Stuck

**1.** **Do you believe two people are fated to be a couple or that it's a matter of chance whom you meet and fall in love with?** Why do you think that? How does your marriage (or other intimate relationship) prove your point? Please give an example to illustrate.

M OST PEOPLE never forget the first glimpse of their future spouse, but as often as it's love at first sight, many a romance takes its own sweet time to warm up. Families' reactions can differ as well, as can the duration – and the bliss-and-hiss -- of the courtship and the engagement period. This chapter also calls forth those exciting – and sometimes gory – wedding plans!

Dust off the old photo album and search through it for photos of your dating period and engagement. See if you can remember how you felt when they were taken.

## Quick Quote

"Who ever loved that loved not at first sight?"

— CHRISTOPHER MARLOWE

## Life-Bit

"So, all right, perhaps it wasn't love at first sight. Vicki, in fact, charges me with not even remembering her from those '70s days when she interned in my Senate office mailroom … a charge to which I plead nolo contendere."

— EDWARD KENNEDY, *The Compass: A Memoir by Edward M. Kennedy*

2. **Tell us about the first time you saw your future spouse.**
What were your first impressions? Please include all the details you can! (Include where, when and possibly what you were wearing and eating!)

_____

_____

_____

_____

_____

_____

_____

_____

_____

_____

_____

_____

_____

_____

_____

_____

_____

_____

_____

## 3. How did the courtship go? Smooth and lightning quick? Bumpy and filled with potholes (and maybe the occasional break-up and reunion)? Please take your time and describe your romance – in detail.

_____

_____

_____

_____

_____

_____

_____

_____

_____

_____

_____

_____

_____

_____

_____

_____

_____

_____

## Today's Tip

Fill in the blanks: During our courtship we would --- and then we would ----.

## Quick Quote

"Love one another and you will be happy. It's as simple and as difficult as that."

— MICHAEL LEUNIG

## Life-Bit

"I remember the instant I fell in love with her. Natalie (Wood) had the most expressive brown eyes, dark and dancing and deep."

— ROBERT J. WAGNER, _Pieces of My Heart: A Memoir_

What song do you associate with the time of the proposal? Can you recall the title? Any lyrics? If no song surfaces, what movie did you see together at that time? How did it reflect your life at the time?

**Quick Quote**

"Getting married is the boldest and most idealistic thing that most of us will ever do."

— MAGGIE GALLAGHER

**Life-Bit**

"Six weeks from the time we met, Joe asked me to marry him. I accepted, understanding that the wedding wouldn't take place until after my graduation."

— MADELEINE ALBRIGHT, *Madame Secretary: A Memoir*

4. **Please tell us about the proposal.** We want to hear all the details! How did you feel the moment the question was out? Did the answer come as a surprise? Why or why not?

_____

_____

_____

_____

_____

_____

_____

_____

_____

_____

_____

_____

_____

_____

_____

_____

_____

_____

_____

_____

_____

_____

5. **Did you give a gift to your fiancé?** Did your fiancé give you one? What were they? Can you describe them? If there was an engagement ring, tell us all about it!

_____

_____

_____

_____

_____

_____

_____

_____

_____

_____

_____

_____

_____

_____

_____

_____

_____

_____

_____

What are the three words that come immediately to mind as your first impression of your mother-in-law? Your father-in-law?

## Quick Quote

"A fiancé is neither this nor that: he's left one shore, but not yet reached the other."

— ANTON CHEKHOV

## Life-Bit

"When Art had to go to the bathroom, I went with him. And there, pissing side by side in our urinals, I said, 'I'd like to marry your daughter.' He said, 'Oh, yeah. Okay.'"

— GEORGE CARLIN, *Last Words: A Memoir*

**6.** **How did you relate to your future in-laws at first?** How did your fiancé relate to your family? Please give specifics, and be honest!

_____

_____

_____

_____

_____

_____

_____

_____

_____

_____

_____

_____

_____

_____

_____

_____

_____

_____

_____

_____

**7.** **How did the families relate to** *each other* **during the engagement period (or later if you eloped)?** Please give a typical example of their interaction.

_____

_____

_____

_____

_____

_____

_____

_____

_____

_____

_____

_____

_____

_____

_____

_____

_____

_____

_____

_____

_____

_____

## Quick Quote

"… he thinks my girlfriends are very childish, and he's quite right."

— ANNE FRANK

## Life-Bit

"Bella (Abzug) was crazy about Phil and taunted me about marrying him. 'What's wrong with you? You think you're going to do better than this?'"

— MARLO THOMAS, *Growing Up Laughing*

**8.** **How did your friends get along with your fiancé?** Any memorable exchanges between them?

_____

_____

_____

_____

_____

_____

_____

_____

_____

_____

_____

_____

_____

_____

_____

_____

_____

_____

_____

**Just remembered something else?**
**Feel free to use your extra pages at the end of this chapter.**

## 9. How long were you engaged?
Why did you pick that timing? Were there any surprises you discovered about your fiancé during the engagement period? If so, please tell us about it.

_____

_____

_____

_____

_____

_____

_____

_____

_____

_____

_____

_____

_____

_____

_____

_____

_____

_____

_____

Did you feel like your vote counted in the wedding plans? On which issues *did* it count? And on which ones was it largely ignored?

## Quick Quote

"Whichever side of the family wins the wedding planning battle, that's who the kids are going to look like."

— DAN SPIRA

## Life-Bit

"… I'm not going to sugarcoat the fact that there were a few moments of eating-icing-straight-from-the-can stress and Lizzie-Borden-took-an-axe rage."

— ELIZABETH WIGGS MAAS, *How I Planned Your Wedding*

**10.** **Who planned your wedding?** Did you all see eye-to-eye or was there a lot of conflict? Please tell us about it, in as much detail as possible!

_____

_____

_____

_____

_____

_____

_____

_____

_____

_____

_____

_____

_____

_____

_____

_____

_____

_____

_____

_____

_____

**11.** **During the planning phase, what was the most important part of the wedding day to you as an individual and as a couple?** The location? The ceremony? The music? The guest-list? The food? Something else? Did you insist on having your way on it? How did that play out?

_____

_____

_____

_____

_____

_____

_____

_____

_____

_____

_____

_____

_____

_____

_____

_____

_____

_____

_____

What was the best piece of wedding planning advice you got? Who gave it? Did you take it … or not? Why?

"As long as the world is turning and spinning, we're gonna be dizzy and we're gonna make mistakes."

— MEL BROOKS

"The plan was to get married at the most expensive hotel in the world, in Kingston, Jamaica … an altercation did erupt a few days before the marriage when I guess I said I didn't want to go through with it. Still, I let myself be swayed."

— LESLIE CARON,
*Thank Heaven: A Memoir*

## 12. If there was one aspect of the wedding planning you would have done differently, what is it? Please tell us what happened and how you think it *could* have turned out had you done things differently!

_____

_____

_____

_____

_____

_____

_____

_____

_____

_____

_____

_____

_____

_____

_____

_____

_____

### Don't Forget to PLET!

**Now return to Chapter 2 to add Pivotal Life Events you remembered during this chapter. You'll be glad you did!!**

LIFEJOURNEY
BOOKS

**1.** **When you close your eyes and think about your wedding day, what image pops up first?** Please describe the scene and how it made you feel.

B Y NOW, MOST OF your contentious issues are resolved and you and your spouse-to-be can enjoy this most wonderful of days – or not! Either way, this chapter will record it all – whether you walked down a flowered aisle, tied the knot at City Hall or learned the hard way that you and your mother-in-law didn't see eye-to-eye. Don't skimp on all the rich and colorful details, this is the stuff that memories are made of, whether you were a traditional bride and groom or you chose to take a different route to committing to the one you love.

Surround yourself with pictures from your wedding.

## Quick Quote

"It took great courage to ask a beautiful young woman to marry me. Believe me, it is easier to play the whole *Petrushka* on the piano."

— ARTHUR RUBINSTEIN

## Life-Bit

"They were married four months later, my father proposing in Le Grande Place, in Brussels, on his way to meet my mother's entire family at her brother's wedding. How narrowly they almost missed each other, and at the same time, how inevitable it was ..."

— VALERIE STEIKER, *The Leopard's Hat: A Daughter's Story*

2. **Were you the first person to get married in your family?**
The last? Was it a big deal? Describe your family's attitude towards the wedding.

_____

_____

_____

_____

_____

_____

_____

_____

_____

_____

_____

_____

_____

_____

_____

_____

_____

_____

_____

## 3. Did the wedding turn out as planned? How or how not? Please provide as many details as you can, referring to your photos for inspiration!

_____

_____

_____

_____

_____

_____

_____

_____

_____

_____

_____

_____

_____

_____

_____

_____

_____

_____

_____

_____

As best you can remember, write out the menu that was served at your wedding. With a friend or one of your children, recreate one of the dishes as closely as possible.

"Don't marry for money; you can borrow it cheaper."

— SCOTTISH PROVERB

"Everyone we love and care about was there. It was as fun and meaningful as we ever could have hoped."

— DREW BARRYMORE, *People Magazine*

4. **Who paid for the wedding?** Please tell us how the decision was made and how it worked out.

_____

_____

_____

_____

_____

_____

_____

_____

_____

_____

_____

_____

_____

_____

_____

_____

_____

_____

_____

_____

**5.** **What were the trends in weddings in your social circle and in your day?** Were they simple or elaborate affairs? Was your wedding luxurious or bare bones or somewhere in between? Please describe it.

_____

_____

_____

_____

_____

_____

_____

_____

_____

_____

_____

_____

_____

_____

_____

_____

_____

_____

_____

_____

On a piece of paper draw what you and your spouse wore to your wedding.

"I chose my wife, as she did her wedding gown, for qualities that would wear well."

— OLIVER GOLDSMITH

"But will I sew her wedding dress? I will. I buy white slipper satin and skeins of white floss. All that spring, in the early mornings, before I go to work, I will sip coffee in the first sunlight while the folds of white satin spill off my lap." '

— MARY CLEARMAN
    BLEW, *Balsamroot:
    A Memoir*

**6.** **Did the bride wear a traditional white gown?** Did the groom wear a tux? Or did you and your spouse opt for something totally different? Describe the garments you chose for this special day. Do you remember why you made the decisions you did? Please share the details.

_____

_____

_____

_____

_____

_____

_____

_____

_____

_____

_____

_____

_____

_____

_____

_____

**7. Who walked you down the aisle?** Was it an emotional moment? Do you remember what you were thinking as you tied the knot with your beloved?

_____

_____

_____

_____

_____

_____

_____

_____

_____

_____

_____

_____

_____

_____

_____

_____

_____

_____

_____

_____

_____

Find the religious documentation of your marriage. Why not preserve and/or display it in a way that will be most meaningful to you?

## Quick Quote

"The secret of a happy marriage remains a secret."

— HENNY YOUNGMAN

## Life-Bit

"When I was about ten, all of us Meyer children were baptized at home to satisfy my devout Lutheran maternal grandmother, who thought that without such a precaution we were all headed for hell. But for the most part, religion was not part of our lives."

— KATHERINE GRAHAM, *Personal History*

## 8. Was your marriage ceremony religious or secular?

Was it important to you, or to your family, to have a religious ceremony? And do you still practice that religion? Please tell us about it.

_____

_____

_____

_____

_____

_____

_____

_____

_____

_____

_____

_____

_____

_____

_____

**Just remembered something else?**
**Feel free to use your extra pages at the end of this chapter.**

## 9. Do you remember the food at your wedding reception?

The speeches? The décor? Were any guests less than sober? Try to describe the scene as best you can with as many details as you can muster!

_____

_____

_____

_____

_____

_____

_____

_____

_____

_____

_____

_____

_____

_____

_____

_____

_____

_____

If you can, talk to someone who was at your wedding. Ask them what *they* remember most from that day. If you can't, please share an experience a guest may have shared with you later.

## Quick Quote

"Gravitation is not responsible for people falling in love."

— ALBERT EINSTEIN

## Life-Bit

"Mick arranged what he saw as a quiet wedding for which he chose Saint-Tropez at the height of the season. No journalist stayed at home."

— KEITH RICHARDS, JAMES FOX, *Life*

## 10. What was the highlight of your wedding day for you?

Please describe that moment with as many details as you can.

_____

_____

_____

_____

_____

_____

_____

_____

_____

_____

_____

_____

_____

_____

_____

_____

_____

_____

## 11. Where did you and your spouse go right after the wedding? Did you go on a honeymoon? Describe the first few days of wedded bliss.

_____

_____

_____

_____

_____

_____

_____

_____

_____

_____

_____

_____

_____

_____

_____

_____

_____

_____

_____

_____

### Today's Tip

Think about it - If you could do your honeymoon all over (and money were no obstacle), where would you go today?

### Quick Quote

"There seems to be an unwritten law that going on honeymoons is like joining the Masons ... secret and mysterious, and the fewer questions asked the less embarrassing for everybody."

— MARTHA BYRD PORTER, _Straight Down a Crooked Lane_

### Life-Bit

"The house that MO occupied with DA was anything but a honeymoon cottage ... it had no indoor plumbing, no running water and no electricity. The two of them shared the house with several cowboys, who slept on the screen porch."

— SANDRA DAY O'CONNOR, H. ALAN DAY, _Lazy B_

## Quick Quote

"Keep your eyes wide open before marriage, half shut afterwards."

— BENJAMIN FRANKLIN

## Life-Bit

"Since we first met, my romantic fella had always had a delicious habit of leaving little love notes for me in unexpected places (I still have them all)…"

— BETTY WHITE,
*If You Ask Me:
(And of Course You Won't)*

**12.** **If you had to do it all over again, would you change anything about your wedding day?** Why or why not? Please describe.

_____

_____

_____

_____

_____

_____

_____

_____

_____

_____

_____

_____

_____

_____

_____

_____

## Don't Forget to PLET!

Now return Chapter 2 to add Pivotal Life Events you remembered during this chapter. You'll be glad you did!!

# 10 Marriage: The Early Years

**1.** **What was your greatest joy in your early marriage years?**
Please tell us about it in detail.

_____

_____

_____

_____

_____

_____

_____

_____

_____

_____

_____

_____

_____

_____

_____

_____

_____

_____

I N THE EARLY months and years of your marriage (or other loving partnership), your commonalities and differences surfaced, at times bringing great joy, at other times difficult challenges. But one thing is certain: Through it all, as you adapted to life together, you changed, as individuals and as a couple. Looking back over the years, the hard-earned secrets of a marriage will be shared, along with those lessons you as a couple had to learn for yourselves. This includes the happiest times as well as the biggest bumps in your marriage – and how they were resolved.

**2.** **What was the hardest lesson you had to learn in the first year of marriage?** How did you accomplish this?

_____

_____

_____

_____

_____

_____

_____

_____

_____

_____

_____

_____

_____

_____

_____

_____

_____

_____

## 3. What was the best marital advice you got? Who gave it to you and when? How did it work for you?

_____

_____

_____

_____

_____

_____

_____

_____

_____

_____

_____

_____

_____

_____

_____

_____

_____

_____

_____

_____

_____

_____

Please sketch the layout of the first home you shared ... Add as many furnishings as you can!

"Marriage should be a duet – when one sings, the other claps."

— JOE MURRAY

"I used to believe that marriage would diminish me, reduce my options, that you had to be someone less to live with someone else when, of course, you have to be more."

— CANDACE BERGEN,
*Knock Wood*

4. **When did you stop thinking in terms of "me" or "I" and start thinking of "we?"** Please give an example. What do you think triggered that transformation?

_____

_____

_____

_____

_____

_____

_____

_____

_____

_____

_____

_____

_____

_____

_____

_____

_____

_____

## 5. What was the biggest surprise in your early marital years?

How did it affect you in positive or negative ways? Can you look back on it with greater clarity now? If so, how has your understanding of it changed?

_____

_____

_____

_____

_____

_____

_____

_____

_____

_____

_____

_____

_____

_____

_____

_____

_____

_____

_____

_____

_____

### Today's Tip

Did your spouse ever surprise you with a gift? Or were you the surprise gift-giver? Either way, name one gift that stands out.

### Quick Quote

"Marriage isn't just spiritual communion and passionate embraces. Marriage is also three meals a day, sharing the workload and remembering to carry out the trash."

— DR. JOYCE BROTHERS

### Life-Bit

"On our wedding night, Desi woke me out of a sound sleep... I thought the hotel must be on fire. "I'm thirsty," he explained. "Please get me a glass of water, darling." I was out of bed and running the tap in the bathroom before I woke up sufficiently to wonder why he didn't get it himself."

— LUCILLE BALL, *Love, Lucy*

Please describe what you would say was the biggest difference between your two families.

"Behind every successful man is a proud wife and a surprised mother-in-law."

— HUBERT H. HUMPHREY

"I liked her (my mother-in-law) a lot ... She's very different than my mother. Melba was very loving, very attentive, sharp and no-nonsense. She was also very kind to me."

— MEREDITH BAXTER, *Untied*

6. **How did you interact with each other's families during these early days of marriage?** Please give examples.

_____

_____

_____

_____

_____

_____

_____

_____

_____

_____

_____

_____

_____

_____

_____

_____

_____

_____

_____

_____

## 7. What was your greatest financial challenge as a couple back then? How did you resolve it?

_____

_____

_____

_____

_____

_____

_____

_____

_____

_____

_____

_____

_____

_____

_____

_____

_____

_____

_____

_____

## Today's Tip

What was the most expensive purchase you made in the first two years of marriage? Did it turn out to be a smart investment? Why or why not?

## Quick Quote

"A good marriage is like a good trade. Each thinks he got the better deal."

— IVERN BALL

## Life-Bit

"We could barely afford a wedding trip. We added up her savings and mine, figuring how much we had to start life, with it coming out to $600 between us."

— ALAN ALDA,
_Never Have Your Dog Stuffed_

Jot down the terms of endearment you called your spouse back then and the one s/he called you. (We promise not to tell!)

## Quick Quote

"Sexiness wears thin after a while and beauty fades, but to be married to a man who makes you laugh every day, ah, now that's a real treat."

— JOANNE WOODWARD

## Life-Bit

"… the first time he (Michael Todd) made love to me, I think my heart stopped beating."

—— ELIZABETH TAYLOR, *A Passion for Life*

## 8. How was the more intimate side of your relationship?

What did you learn from that part of your marriage?

_____

_____

_____

_____

_____

_____

_____

_____

_____

_____

_____

_____

_____

_____

_____

_____

_____

_____

_____

_____

**Just remembered something else?**
**Feel free to use your extra pages at the end of this chapter.**

## 9. What was the best time in your marriage in these early years? Why? Please share a story that reflects that.

_____

_____

_____

_____

_____

_____

_____

_____

_____

_____

_____

_____

_____

_____

_____

_____

_____

_____

_____

_____

"Do not marry a man to reform him. That is what reform schools are for. "

— MAE WEST

"…when he was drunk he would use the worst of oaths. I don't mention this to expose my husband, but to show the effect it had on me, for I now saw myself ruined as I thought, joined to a man I had no love for…"

— GEORGE SAND, *Story of My Life*

**10.** **How did you have to change to stay happy in the marriage?** How did your spouse?

_____

_____

_____

_____

_____

_____

_____

_____

_____

_____

_____

_____

_____

_____

_____

_____

_____

_____

_____

## 11. What was one of the hardest lessons of your marriage?

Why do you think that was? If you resolved it, how did you do it?
If not, why not?

_____

_____

_____

_____

_____

_____

_____

_____

_____

_____

_____

_____

_____

_____

_____

_____

_____

_____

## Today's Tip

List the three most difficult challenges you faced in these early years.

## Quick Quote

"I have learned that only two things are necessary to keep one's wife happy. First, let her think she's having her own way. And, second, let her have it."

— LYNDON B. JOHNSON

## Life-Bit

"… it's not that I was a terrible person but admittedly almost always I put my responsibilities ahead of the relationship. I could justify it in my mind; my career financed the relationship. But I've learned; oh I've learned."

— WILLIAM SHATNER, _Up Till Now: The Autobiography_

Turn the tables and speak as if you were your spouse, giving you a typical lecture. What is s/he saying?

## Quick Quote

"Where there is love there is life."

— MAHATMA GANDHI

## Life-Bit

"A successful marriage requires falling in love many times, always with the same person."

— MIGNON MCLAUGHLIN

# 12. Looking back, what did you learn from your spouse (or significant other) about how to live? How did that change your life?

_____

_____

_____

_____

_____

_____

_____

_____

_____

_____

_____

_____

_____

_____

_____

_____

## Don't Forget to PLET!

Now return to Chapter 2 to add Pivotal Life Events that you remembered during this chapter. You'll be glad you did!!

# 11 Here Come the Kids! Becoming a Parent

**1.** **Was the first pregnancy a surprise?** Was it planned? How did you find out you were going to become a parent? How did you feel at that moment? Please tell us all about it.

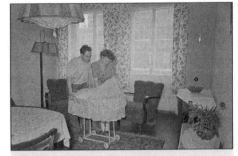

_____

_____

_____

_____

_____

_____

_____

_____

_____

_____

_____

_____

_____

_____

_____

_____

_____

_____

_____

_____

B ECOMING A parent is like nothing you have ever experienced before. Suddenly, you are responsible for more than just yourselves. Your adjustment to this major new role probably involved joy, frustration, exhaustion, humor and infinite humility. Whether your parenthood came about through a birth or an adoption, those early years with small children brought sleepless nights, small bottoms to wipe, little fingers clinging to your neck and "I love you's" that took your breath away.

Dig out the baby pictures for each of your children and set them up on the table where you are working. Be sure to sneak peeks at them while answering these questions.

"Childbirth is more admirable than conquest, more amazing than self-defense, and as courageous as either one."

— GLORIA STEINEM

"I was a much longed-for baby. It wasn't for want of trying that my parents were childless for so long."

— MADELEINE L'ENGLE, *The Summer Of The Great-Grandmother*

2. **Tell the 'birth story' for each of your children's births.**
Don't leave out any details and pay special attention to the most memorable moments.

_____

_____

_____

_____

_____

_____

_____

_____

_____

_____

_____

_____

_____

_____

_____

_____

_____

_____

_____

_____

_____

_____

## 3. What is the story behind each of your children's names?

Was it easy to choose or contentious? Please tell us about the entire name-selection story for each one.

_____

_____

_____

_____

_____

_____

_____

_____

_____

_____

_____

_____

_____

_____

_____

_____

_____

_____

_____

_____

_____

### Today's Tip

If you were going to name a child today, what might those names be and why?

### Quick Quote

"Rembrandt's first name was Beauregard, which is why he never used it."

—DAVE BARRY

### Life-Bit

"Mary Catherine Bateson was born on December 8, 1939, and looked very much herself."

—MARGARET MEAD, *Blackberry Winter, My Earlier Years*

What is the best parenting tip you would want to pass on to your children and grandchildren?

"The trouble with learning to parent on the job is that your child is the teacher."

— ROBERT BRAULT

"Children inherit the qualities of the parents, no less than their physical features. Environment does play an important part, but the original capital on which a child starts in life is inherited from its ancestors."

— MAHATMA GHANDI, *An Autobiography: The Story of My Experiments With Truth*

## 4. What was the hardest adjustment you had to make in your new role as a parent? How did you adapt? Please give a concrete – and detailed – example.

_____

_____

_____

_____

_____

_____

_____

_____

_____

_____

_____

_____

_____

_____

_____

_____

_____

_____

**5.** **Were you home every day or kissing the baby goodbye every morning or something in between?** Describe your daily routine with your babies.

_____

_____

_____

_____

_____

_____

_____

_____

_____

_____

_____

_____

_____

_____

_____

_____

_____

_____

_____

_____

Are you still in touch with friends from these early days of parenthood? Give a call, drop a note or do a Google search (with help, if need be) to try to reconnect with them and remember those times together.

## Quick Quote

"Parenthood is a lot easier to get into than out of."

— BRUCE LANSKY

## Life-Bit

"Chester was the heart of her life, and like many another mother, she economized that her son should have 'his chance'."

— ANONYMOUS,
*The Highroad Being the Autobiography of an Ambitious Mother*

6. **Who did you spend time with, and who kept you sane, in those crazy first months of parenthood?** Please record a typical conversation (as best you can remember) and describe the kind of activity you did together, even if it's just sharing the morning coffee and newspaper at your kitchen table.

_____

_____

_____

_____

_____

_____

_____

_____

_____

_____

_____

_____

_____

_____

_____

_____

**7.** **Did you enjoy your children's "babyhood" or were you eager for them to get bigger and be less dependent?** If you had more than one, did that feeling change with each additional child? Please describe an aspect of the "babyhood" that you particularly enjoyed.

_____

_____

_____

_____

_____

_____

_____

_____

_____

_____

_____

_____

_____

_____

_____

_____

_____

_____

_____

_____

## Today's Tip

Write down one thing that was distinctive about each of your babies. Was it the way they sucked their thumb? Slept through any noise? Screamed with colic? Then share the list with your children and see what _they_ recall.

## Quick Quote

"But the hearts of small children are delicate organs. A cruel beginning in this world can twist them into curious shapes."

— CARSON MCCULLERS

## Life-Bit

"My parents had early given me religious impressions and brought me through my childhood piously in the Dissenting way."

— BENJAMIN FRANKLIN, _Autobiography_

**www.LifeJourneyBooks.com**

"When my kids become wild and unruly, I use a nice, safe playpen. When they're finished, I climb out."

— ERMA BOMBECK

"Her mother followed a custom not unusual in those days of putting out her babies to be nursed in a cottage in a village. The infant was visited daily by one or both of its parents and frequently brought to them at the parsonage, but the cottage was its home."

— JAMES EDWARD AUSTEN LEIGH, *A Memoir of Jane Austen*

**8. Please tell us about two of your most memorable moments as a brand new parent.** Don't skimp on the details – from the delightful to the gruesome.

_____

_____

_____

_____

_____

_____

_____

_____

_____

_____

_____

_____

_____

_____

_____

_____

_____

_____

_____

**Just remembered something else?**
**Feel free to use your extra pages at the end of this chapter.**

**9.** **How did your relationship with your parents change once you became a parent?** Your in-laws? How would you describe each of them as grandparents?

_____

_____

_____

_____

_____

_____

_____

_____

_____

_____

_____

_____

_____

_____

_____

_____

_____

_____

_____

## Quick Quote

"There are two lasting bequests we can give our children. One is roots. The other is wings."

— HODDING CARTER, JR.

## Life-Bit

"I am now the father of three sons. I have very little knowledge or curiosity of what they think of me. They are always polite. I have tried to fulfill the same duties to them and provide the same amusements as my father did to me."

— ALEXANDER WAUGH, *Fathers and Sons: The Autobiography of a Family*

**10.** **How would you describe yours and your spouse's parenting styles?** Who was the worrier? The disciplinarian? The softie? Please give examples to illustrate.

_____

_____

_____

_____

_____

_____

_____

_____

_____

_____

_____

_____

_____

_____

_____

_____

_____

_____

**11.** **Did you have a traditional approach to parenting roles or not?** Were you both satisfied with that or did it create conflict in your marriage? Please describe.

_____

_____

_____

_____

_____

_____

_____

_____

_____

_____

_____

_____

_____

_____

_____

_____

_____

_____

_____

_____

_____

_____

If you had one adjective to describe each of your babies what would it be?

"Don't forget that compared to a grownup person every baby is a genius. Think of the capacity to learn! The freshness, the temperament, the will of a baby a few months old!"

— MAY SARTON

"And when our baby stirs and struggles to be born it compels humility: what we began is now its own."

—— MARGARET MEAD

**12.** **How did your babies grow?** Please describe a memorable milestone from the miraculous ever-changing first year with each of your babies.

_____

_____

_____

_____

_____

_____

_____

_____

_____

_____

_____

_____

_____

_____

_____

## Don't Forget to PLET!

Now return to Chapter 2 to add Pivotal Life Events you remembered during this chapter. You'll be glad you did!!

**1.** Tell us about each one of the children, describing them as they grew.

THIS CHAPTER provides the chance to explore each child's unique impact on the family and on you, as well as an invitation to share something about each one, a story revealing the special person he or she was destined to become. We're also going to ask you to share some of your parenting highlights as well as those things you now wish you had done somewhat differently.

## Tip

*Please note: If you don't have children, please answer the questions as they pertain to you – concerning especially beloved nieces, nephews, stepchildren, godchildren, etc.*

From your perspective as a mature adult, ask yourself if you had one thing you could say to your mother about her role as a mother, what would it be? Your dad?

## Quick Quote

"We never know the love of our parents for us till we have become parents."

— HENRY WARD BEECHER

## Life-Bit

"I am more proud of my daughter than I could possibly express. She's a beautiful, delightful, funny woman. She marches to her own drummer."

— BARBARA WALTERS, *Audition: A Memoir*

2. **How was your own parenting style similar to your parents' style?** How was it different? Please give examples to illustrate.

## 3. Which of your children are more like you? In what ways? Please give us details to illustrate.

_____

_____

_____

_____

_____

_____

_____

_____

_____

_____

_____

_____

_____

_____

_____

_____

_____

_____

_____

Close your eyes and think back over the years. Then name one word for the role your spouse played in each child's life, ie protector, motivator, muse, etc.

## Quick Quote

"His heritage to his children wasn't words or possessions, but an unspoken treasure, the treasure of his example as a man and a father."

— WILL ROGERS JR.

## Life-Bit

"Todd grabbed the birth certificate before I could get to it, declaring that his first daughter would be named "Bristol" ... for the bay he'd loved since childhood."

— SARAH PALIN,
*Going Rogue:
An American Life*

4. **Which of your children are more like your spouse?** In what ways? Please give real-life examples.

_____

_____

_____

_____

_____

_____

_____

_____

_____

_____

_____

_____

_____

_____

_____

_____

_____

_____

_____

_____

**5.** **What was your proudest moment(s) as a parent?** Please paint the picture for us in sights, sounds, smells and feelings. Why does it stand out?

_____

_____

_____

_____

_____

_____

_____

_____

_____

_____

_____

_____

_____

_____

_____

_____

_____

_____

_____

_____

## Today's Tip

Please fill in the blank: I enjoyed parenthood because ----.

## Quick Quote

"Yes, having a child is surely the most beautifully irrational act that two people in love can commit."

-BILL COSBY

## Life-Bit

"I think what surprised me the most about motherhood, as sentimental as it sounds, is how much I love my kids. I mean, I just can't believe it. It's like a whole new dimension in emotion that I've never experienced."

— GWYNETH PALTROW

www.LifeJourneyBooks.com

Describe your approach to discipline in animal terms, ie were you an Irish setter, a giraffe, a cheetah? And why?

"Every parent is at some time the father of the unreturned prodigal, with nothing to do but keep his house open to hope."

— JOHN CIARDI

"My children were on my mind, each time I came up and each time I went back down. I worried about how they would get an education, how they would manage … how would my family react back in Nassau when they'd heard I'd drowned?"

— SIDNEY POITIER, *The Measure of a Man: A Spiritual Autobiography*

6. **What was your hardest moment as a parent?** Why? Please describe it in detail.

_____

_____

_____

_____

_____

_____

_____

_____

_____

_____

_____

_____

_____

_____

_____

_____

_____

## 7. How would you describe yourself as a parent? Your spouse? Please illustrate with an example for each of you.

_____

_____

_____

_____

_____

_____

_____

_____

_____

_____

_____

_____

_____

_____

_____

_____

_____

_____

_____

_____

If each of your children had led a previous life, briefly describe what he or she would have been.

"By the time a man realizes that maybe his father was right, he usually has a son who thinks he's wrong."

— CHARLES WADSWORTH

"Poor, tired child. How she loved her life, how longingly and eagerly she clung to it through all those twenty-two months of captivity and loneliness and bodily suffering. And how pathetically she searched our eyes for hope."

— MARK TWAIN, *The Autobiography of Mark Twain*

**8.** Tell us one story about each child that reveals something about the adult they were destined to become.

_____

_____

_____

_____

_____

_____

_____

_____

_____

_____

_____

_____

_____

_____

_____

_____

_____

**Just remembered something else?**
**Feel free to use your extra pages at the end of this chapter.**

## 9. What's the best lesson you taught your children about life? What was your spouse's best lesson to the children? Please give an example of each.

_____

_____

_____

_____

_____

_____

_____

_____

_____

_____

_____

_____

_____

_____

_____

_____

_____

_____

_____

Do you recall any of your children sharing with you any childhood confidences? If so, please jot down what you can recall. (Don't worry if it's not the exact wording!)

## Quick Quote

"It is the malady of our age that the young are so busy teaching us that they have no time left to learn."

— ERIC HOFFER

## Life-Bit

"Life was give-and-take. What we'd gotten in return as parents was much bigger than whatever we'd sacrificed."

— TORI SPELLING, *Unchartered Territories*

## 10. What's the best lesson each of your children taught *you* about life? Please illustrate each lesson with an example.

_____

_____

_____

_____

_____

_____

_____

_____

_____

_____

_____

_____

_____

_____

_____

_____

_____

_____

_____

**11.** **How is it different being a parent now than when you were raising children?** Please share examples from your life.

_____

_____

_____

_____

_____

_____

_____

_____

_____

_____

_____

_____

_____

_____

_____

_____

_____

_____

### Today's Tip

Name three things that have _not_ changed about parenthood.

### Quick Quote

"My instinct is to protect my children from pain. But adversity is often the thing that gives us character and backbone. It's always been a struggle for me to back off and let my children go through difficult experiences."

—— NICOLE KIDMAN

### Life-Bit

"Unfortunately in those days fathers weren't present for births and they couldn't even see their babies right after they were born. And so, when they finally brought Patti in to me, I was alone. I so would have liked to share the moment with Ronnie."

— NANCY REAGAN,
_I Love You, Ronnie_

12. **If you could give** *each child* **one piece of advice now, what would it be?** Please list each child's name alongside your advice for each.

_____

_____

_____

_____

_____

_____

_____

_____

_____

_____

_____

_____

_____

_____

_____

_____

_____

_____

### Don't Forget to PLET!

Now return to Chapter 2 to add Pivotal Life Events you remembered during this chapter. You'll be glad you did!!

**1.** **What did you set off into adulthood expecting your career to be?** Did it go as planned? Please tell us why or why not and provide a few details.

_____

_____

_____

_____

_____

_____

_____

_____

_____

_____

_____

_____

_____

_____

_____

_____

_____

_____

_____

F OR SOME OF us a job is fundamentally the means to put food on the table and cover our bills – in other words, a paycheck. For others it's a true passion, an expression of an inner drive and identity. Or, at the very least, it plays a big role in defining our sense of self. This chapter will explore where your career path took you and the role work plays in _your_ life journey. Note: If your job was full-time homemaker, please reflect on the role you played in your spouse's career.

Name the three top career choices you had as a youngster.

"Whatever you can do, or dream you can, begin it … Boldness has genius, power, and magic in it."

— GOETHE

"I can remember very clearly my father saying … 'the thing about being a dancer is that before you get to forty probably you won't be able to go on dancing.' Until then I was really quite serious about wanting to be a ballet dancer."

— JUDI DENCH,
*Scenes From My Life*

2. **What was your first real job?** How did you get it? How long did you last on that job? Please describe the experience.

_____

_____

_____

_____

_____

_____

_____

_____

_____

_____

_____

_____

_____

_____

_____

_____

_____

_____

_____

_____

**3.** **How did your work life dovetail with your family obligations?** Was it a challenge? If so, why was it difficult and how did you deal with it?

_____

_____

_____

_____

_____

_____

_____

_____

_____

_____

_____

_____

_____

_____

_____

_____

_____

_____

_____

_____

_____

## Today's Tip

Sketch a floor plan of your first real job's workplace, be it an office, store, the cab of a truck, etc.

## Quick Quote

"Many people limit themselves to what they think they can do. You can go as far as your mind lets you. What you believe, you can achieve."

— MARY KAY ASH

## Life-Bit

"The Vann-Kennedy job may have been one of the best breaks of my life. But it was also the beginning of the end of my college education, a matter I have regretted ever since. At the time, though, I found the Texas legislature and the newspaper business far more fascinating…"

— WALTER CRONKITE,
_A Reporter's Life_

www.LifeJourneyBooks.com

When you think back to your morning routine when your children were small, who was the first one out of the house? Where were they heading?

## Quick Quote

"What's so great about work anyway? Work won't visit you when you're old."

— TINA FEY

## Life-Bit

"I [balance work with raising 2 kids] with great precision. I plan everything in advance: who's picking up. We have charts, maps and lists on the fridge, all over the house. I sometimes feel like I'm with the CIA."

— KATE WINSLET

4. **Please describe an enduring friendship you made on the job.** How did that relationship impact your life at the time? Your career?

_____

_____

_____

_____

_____

_____

_____

_____

_____

_____

_____

_____

_____

_____

_____

_____

_____

_____

_____

## 5. What were your proudest accomplishments on the job?

Please tell us about the job that best defined you and why.

_____

_____

_____

_____

_____

_____

_____

_____

_____

_____

_____

_____

_____

_____

_____

_____

_____

_____

_____

_____

_____

_____

Close your eyes and think of several people you consider successful in their careers. Then jot down in 20 words or less, what you believe their secret to success is.

## Quick Quote

"Believe in yourself! Have faith in your abilities! Without a humble but reasonable confidence in your own powers you cannot be successful or happy."

— NORMAN VINCENT PEALE

## Life-Bit

"I wasn't supposed to live after getting blown up by a grenade … but I did and once I got back, I just kept making it a little further. No one thought that I'd learn to walk again. Or swim. Or drive. Or get elected to the United States Senate. The only way to get over the obstacles for me is to keep pressing a need."

— MAX CLELAND, *Heart of a Patriot*

6. **When did you feel most fulfilled at work and why?** Please describe a typical day on that job.

_____

_____

_____

_____

_____

_____

_____

_____

_____

_____

_____

_____

_____

_____

_____

_____

_____

## 7. When in your career were you most frustrated? Looking back on it, why do you think that was? How was the situation resolved? How did you feel about it then and, looking back over the years, how do you see that period now?

_____

_____

_____

_____

_____

_____

_____

_____

_____

_____

_____

_____

_____

_____

_____

_____

_____

_____

_____

Did you ever feel like giving up on your dream? What kept you going?

"Character cannot be developed in ease and quiet. Only through experiences of trial and suffering can the soul be strengthened, vision cleared, ambition inspired and success achieved."

— HELEN KELLER

"After the impeachment ordeal, people often asked me how I got through it without losing my mind, or at least the ability to keep doing the job."

— BILL CLINTON, *My Life*

**8.** **How has the workaday world changed since you first entered the workplace?** Is this a positive or negative change and why?

_____

_____

_____

_____

_____

_____

_____

_____

_____

_____

_____

_____

_____

_____

_____

_____

_____

_____

_____

**Just remembered something else?**
**Feel free to use your extra pages at the end of this chapter.**

## 9. How has *your* **field changed over the years?** How has it stayed the same? Please provide examples.

_____

_____

_____

_____

_____

_____

_____

_____

_____

_____

_____

_____

_____

_____

_____

_____

_____

_____

_____

"The most familiar people stand each moment in some new relation to each other, to their work, to surrounding objects."

— HENRY WARD BEECHER

"There's a bunch of new values, there are many new values. There's a bunch of new people who were born of them and the blood of many heroes."

— FIDEL CASTRO, *My Life*

**10.** **Did you ever give a younger person (other than your children) a helping hand in their career?** Please tell us about it.

**11.** **What were the career roads not taken?** How did you make that decision? Looking back, are you glad your career turned out as it did or do you have any regrets? Why?

_____

_____

_____

_____

_____

_____

_____

_____

_____

_____

_____

_____

_____

_____

_____

_____

_____

_____

_____

Who was your mentor? What main lesson did that person teach you? Please describe both the relationship and its impact.

## Quick Quote

"A mentor is someone who allows you to see the hope inside yourself."

— OPRAH WINFREY

## Life-Bit

"Ray Charles is a giant. He was my mentor. He would write arrangements in Braille and translate it to me."

— QUINCY JONES,
_The Autobiography of Quincy Jones_

What would you have missed out on had your original career goals taken shape?

"Yet knowing how way leads on to way, I doubted if I should ever come back."

— ROBERT FROST

"If I had been free of my middle-class entanglements, my family, my house, my debt structure, my obligations, this might have been the point where I veered off into conceptual art."

— GEORGE CARLIN, *Last Words: A Memoir*

$12.$ **What advice would you give a young person just starting out in your field today?** Why is that an important thing to remember?

_____

_____

_____

_____

_____

_____

_____

_____

_____

_____

_____

_____

_____

_____

_____

_____

**Don't Forget to PLET!**

Now return to Chapter 2 to add Pivotal Life Events you remembered during this chapter. You'll be glad you did!!

**1.** **When did you first meet your closest lifetime friend?**
Please tell the story of that first encounter.

_____

_____

_____

_____

_____

_____

_____

_____

_____

_____

W HETHER this person is a childhood pal, long-time roommate or the friend you made when your children were little, there's so much that's been shared between best friends that a chapter deserves to be devoted to this special relationship. Here's a chance to explore and remember just what held you together for so long and so well. If you can't limit yourself to one, that's OK – use the extra pages to describe your most significant friendships.

_____

_____

_____

_____

_____

_____

_____

_____

_____

Gather up any mementoes you have of experiences shared with your best friend. They can be ticket stubs, photo booth pictures, or restaurant receipts – anything that will remind you of wonderful times spent together.

## Quick Quote

"Many people will walk in and out of your life, but only true friends will leave footprints in your heart."

— ELEANOR ROOSEVELT

## Life-Bit

"The language of friendship is not words but meanings. It is an intelligence above language. One imagines endless conversations with his Friend in which the tongue shall be loosed and thoughts be spoken without hesitancy or end; but the experience is commonly far otherwise."

— HENRY DAVID THOREAU, *Of Friendship: An Essay From a Week on the Concord and Merrimack Rivers*

**2. Did you get along right away?** What drew you to each other? What kept you together? Please provide examples to illustrate.

_____

_____

_____

_____

_____

_____

_____

_____

_____

_____

_____

_____

_____

_____

_____

_____

_____

_____

**3.** **Did you live near your best friend at one point?** How did you keep in touch? Were you daily phone callers? Letter writers? Please give an example of the lengths you went to in order to stay in touch.

_____

_____

_____

_____

_____

_____

_____

_____

_____

_____

_____

_____

_____

_____

_____

_____

_____

_____

If you could call up your best friend today and tell him or her the one thing you valued most about your friendship, what would it be? (If you can, go ahead and call and tell them!)

## Quick Quote

"Lots of people want to ride with you in the limo, but what you want is someone who will take the bus with you when the limo breaks down."

— OPRAH WINFREY

## Life-Bit

"Mummy's and Margo's natures are completely strange to me. I can understand my friends better than my own mother – too bad!"

— ANNE FRANK, *The Diary of Anne Frank*

4. **Has your best friend understood you in a way no one else ever has?** Please explain and give an example.

_____

_____

_____

_____

_____

_____

_____

_____

_____

_____

_____

_____

_____

_____

_____

_____

_____

_____

_____

**5.** **Did your lives follow similar paths?** Radically different ones? Or somewhere in between? Describe how the course of your lives affected your relationship.

_____

_____

_____

_____

_____

_____

_____

_____

_____

_____

_____

_____

_____

_____

_____

_____

_____

_____

_____

_____

Gather up all the pictures you have of you and your friend. Create an album that you can enjoy and, if possible, share.

"Fear makes strangers of people who would be friends."

— SHIRLEY MACLAINE

"His friendships were few but extremely loyal. He was competitive, difficult, and sometimes impossible with friends and colleagues. When wronged, he never forgot, and when he disliked someone, he relished making their lives miserable."

— BROOKE NEWMAN,
*Jenniemae & James: A Memoir in Black & White*

**6.** **Did you ever experience conflict with your friend?** Describe it – and how you solved the problem (if you did!).

_____

_____

_____

_____

_____

_____

_____

_____

_____

_____

_____

_____

_____

_____

_____

_____

_____

**7.** **Please describe the dynamics of the relationship between you and your best friend.** Who is the strong one? The funny one? The one that leans? The one that gets leaned on? Kindly share a few examples.

_____

_____

_____

_____

_____

_____

_____

_____

_____

_____

_____

_____

_____

_____

_____

_____

_____

_____

_____

_____

Get together with your friend if you can and relive a favorite outing - go to the movies, a café, a ball game – whatever it is that the two of you have often enjoyed doing together.

## Quick Quote

"The real test of friendship is: can you literally do nothing with the other person? Can you enjoy those moments of life that are utterly simple?"

— EUGENE KENNEDY

## Life-Bit

"From girlish giggles to lusty, knowing laughs, laughter has always been present in our friendship. In fact it is one of the keys to our friendship. When Sara's eyes flash with a certain sparkle, I know what she's thinking and I laugh."

— SARA JAMES, GINGER MAUNEY, *The Best of Friends: Two Women, Two Continents, and One Enduring Friendship*

**8. What did you two enjoy most together?** Describe in as much detail as possible one of your best times together.

_____

_____

_____

_____

_____

_____

_____

_____

_____

_____

_____

_____

_____

_____

_____

_____

**Just remembered something else?**
**Feel free to use your extra pages at the end of this chapter.**

**9.** **How has your best friend been there for you in your darkest hour?** Were they a source of comfort? Please tell us about it with as many details as you can muster.

_____

_____

_____

_____

_____

_____

_____

_____

_____

_____

_____

_____

_____

_____

_____

_____

_____

_____

_____

_____

_____

_____

_____

## Life-Bit

"A boy in a schoolyard is called stinky. James, his friend, defends the boy's honor. It's just one responsibility among many. As James and Jeremy grow older, there will also be the responsibility to listen, to anticipate, to remember, to share, to forgive, to overlook, to just plain be there."

— BETH KEPHART,
*Into the Tangle of Friendship:
A Memoir of the
Things That Matter*

**10. Were you able to be there for your best friend when things were tough for them?** Please describe the situation.

## 11. Why do you think you remained connected to your best friend? Please describe what it was about the bond between you that kept you close over the years and please give a few examples!

_____

_____

_____

_____

_____

_____

_____

_____

_____

_____

_____

_____

_____

_____

_____

_____

_____

_____

_____

_____

### Today's Tip

Did you and your spouse have "couple" friends? How did you enjoy spending time together? Write down your most memorable outing with a couple you were close to.

### Quick Quote

"I don't need a friend who changes when I change and who nods when I nod; my shadow does that much better."

— PLUTARCH

### Life-Bit

"… Even while the man was becoming my best friend, I did not know if Mickey had a last name but I found out that Mickey's first name was Talmadge. If you knew what was good for you, you never called him that. Maybe this was because the scourge of the colored people in Georgia was the die-hard segregationist Herman Eugene Talmadge, the state's governor until his death in 1945."

— BERTIE BOWMAN, *Step by Step: A Memoir of Hope, Friendship, Perseverance, and Living the American Dream*

Write a letter to your friend telling them what their friendship has meant to you. Mail it or email it, if possible.

## Quick Quote

"Wishing to be friends is quick work, but friendship is a slow ripening fruit."

— ARISTOTLE

## Life-Bit

"I drew support from my friendship with Mariam and even wondered that when I first met the family I had not paid her much attention … she was intelligent and subtle, and I found beauty in her high cheek-bones and slanting eyes."

— VERONICA DOUBLEDAY, *Three Women of Herat: A Memoir of Life, Love and Friendship in Afghanistan*

12. **How did this friend change you and change your life?**

How would your life be poorer for the lack of your friend? Please give examples.

_____

_____

_____

_____

_____

_____

_____

_____

_____

_____

_____

_____

_____

_____

## Don't Forget to PLET!

**Now return to Chapter 2 to add Pivotal Life Events you remembered during this chapter. You'll be glad you did!!**

# More About Me:
## My Interests & Hobbies

**1.** **As a child, what were you passionate about?** Dancing? Writing? Athletics? Being a fireman? Did your passion translate into a career or a hobby? Please tell us about it.

_____

_____

_____

_____

_____

_____

_____

_____

_____

_____

_____

_____

_____

_____

_____

_____

_____

_____

_____

A S YOUR FAMILY grew and your career - if you worked outside the home - evolved, often in surprising directions, it is what you did just because you *wanted* to that goes a long way toward defining not only many of your greatest joys and satisfactions but also who you are. It could be painting, woodworking, writing poetry, a beloved sport, fishing or spending hours in the garden - whatever it is, it is a truly vital to who you are.

Dig out your old fishing pole, the painting you worked hardest on, a picture of your most prized orchid – anything that reminds you of your best times doing what you have loved to do.

## Quick Quote

"Hobbies of any kind are boring except to people who have the same hobby. This is also true of religion, although you will not find me saying so in print."

— DAVE BARRY

## Life-Bit

"I can elect something I love and absorb myself in it."

— ANAÏS NIN,
*The Diary of Anaïs Nin,
Vol. 1: 1931-1934*

2. **Do you have an interest or a hobby that followed you through the years?** Whether it is coin collecting, car racing or history, describe how you approached this interest in your 20s, your 40s and how you may be expressing that interest now.

_____

_____

_____

_____

_____

_____

_____

_____

_____

_____

_____

_____

_____

_____

_____

_____

_____

_____

3. **Are your interests varied?** Describe some of the ideas and activities you pursued over the years and why (and how) they stuck (or didn't).

_____

_____

_____

_____

_____

_____

_____

_____

_____

_____

_____

_____

_____

_____

_____

_____

_____

_____

Think about all the involvements and hobbies you pursued over the years. Make a list of the top three that brought you the most satisfaction.

**Quick Quote**

"Use what talents you possess; the woods would be very silent if no birds sang except those that sang best."

— HENRY VAN DYKE

**Life-Bit**

"Legendary innovators like Franklin, Snow, and Darwin all possess some common intellectual qualities—a certain quickness of mind, unbounded curiosity—but they also share one other defining attribute. They have a lot of hobbies."

— STEVEN JOHNSON, *Where Good Ideas Come From: The Natural History of Innovation*

Do you still have the old set of golf clubs that you don't use? Old basketballs? Bicycles? An old sewing machine? Think about donating the equipment you don't use anymore to a local charity or give it to someone whom you know would appreciate it.

## Quick Quote

"When love and skill work together, expect a masterpiece."

— JOHN RUSKIN

## Life-Bit

"It is an axiom that no hobby should either seek or need rational justification. To wish to do it is reason enough. To find reasons why it is useful or beneficial converts it at once from an avocation into an industry—lowers it at once to the ignominious category of an 'exercise' undertaken for health, power, or profit."

— ALDO LEOPOLD, *A Sand County Almanac*

## 4. Did any of your interests evolve into something more?

A business? A charity? A full-time pursuit? Please describe.

_____

_____

_____

_____

_____

_____

_____

_____

_____

_____

_____

_____

_____

_____

_____

_____

_____

_____

_____

_____

**5.** **Did you develop relationships with peers who shared your interests?** Describe those you became closest to and how you shared them.

_____

_____

_____

_____

_____

_____

_____

_____

_____

_____

_____

_____

_____

_____

_____

_____

_____

_____

_____

_____

_____

Does your spouse have his/her own interests and hobbies? What are they?

"Men are my hobby. If I ever got married I'd have to give it up."

— MAE WEST

"The only insult I've ever received in my adult life was when someone asked me, "Do you have a hobby?" A HOBBY?! DO I LOOK LIKE A @#$!%$# DABBLER?!"

— JOHN WATERS, *Role Models*

**6.** **Did your spouse or partner share your interest?** Did they tolerate it? Did it bring you closer, create conflict in your relationship or both? Please describe how it happened.

_____

_____

_____

_____

_____

_____

_____

_____

_____

_____

_____

_____

_____

_____

_____

_____

_____

_____

_____

_____

## 7. Did you share your interests with your children? Or someone close to you? In what way? Please describe.

_____

_____

_____

_____

_____

_____

_____

_____

_____

_____

_____

_____

_____

_____

_____

_____

_____

_____

_____

_____

_____

"An artist is only an ordinary man with a greater potentiality – same stuff, same make up, only more force. And the strong driving force usually finds his weak spot, and he goes cranked, or goes under."

— D. H. LAWRENCE

"Never mind that the *habitant* hero of the day, the suddenly incomparable Stoneman, was born in Oak Park, Illinois, and bred at Antonio Junior College in Walnut California; his hobbies, like those of many a red-blooded *Canadian*, were golf and fishing."

— MORDECAI RICHLER, *Dispatches From the Sporting Life*

**8.** **Did your interests bring out the best in you or the worst?**
How? Please provide some examples.

_____

_____

_____

_____

_____

_____

_____

_____

_____

_____

_____

_____

_____

_____

_____

_____

_____

**Just remembered something else?**
**Feel free to use your extra pages at the end of this chapter.**

**9.** **How far did you go in pursuing your interests?** Buying a second home so you could ski? Investing in works of art? Taking off a week from work to go on a fishing trip? Please describe.

_____

_____

_____

_____

_____

_____

_____

_____

_____

_____

_____

_____

_____

_____

_____

_____

_____

_____

_____

_____

_____

_____

### Today's Tip

Watch a movie that involves or invokes your hobby.

### Quick Quote

"When your hobbies get in the way of your work - that's OK; but when your hobbies get in the way of themselves ... well."

— STEVE MARTIN

### Life-Bit

"I hadn't realized how many arcane pursuits there were out in the suburbs."

— ROBERT DREWE, *The Shark Net*

www.LifeJourneyBooks.com

Has the pursuit of your interest changed over the years? How different would it be if you were just starting out now? Please describe.

## Quick Quote

"The profound difference that divides the human race is a question of bait--whether to fish with worms or not."

— VIRGINIA WOOLF

## Life-Bit

"The two men sat silent for a little, and then Lord Peter said: 'D'you like your job?' The detective considered the question, and replied: 'Yes—yes, I do. I know it to be useful, and I am fitted to it. I do it quite well—not with inspiration, perhaps, but sufficiently well to take a pride in it. It is full of variety and it forces one to keep up to the mark and not get slack. And there's a future to it. Yes, I like it. Why?' 'Oh, nothing,' said Peter. 'It's a hobby to me, you see.'"

— DOROTHY L. SAYERS, *Whose Body?*

## 10. Why do you think you pursued the interests you did?
Please explain.

_____

_____

_____

_____

_____

_____

_____

_____

_____

_____

_____

_____

_____

_____

_____

_____

**11.** Please describe in some detail the joy your hobbies and interests brought you over the years. Please give at least one example.

_____

_____

_____

_____

_____

_____

_____

_____

_____

_____

_____

_____

_____

_____

_____

_____

_____

_____

_____

_____

Do a Google search of the most prominent figures in your area of interest. (Please ask for help, if you need it.) What became of them?

### Quick Quote

"The trouble with gardening is that it does not remain an avocation. It becomes an obsession."

— PHYLLIS MCGINLEY

### Life-Bit

"To be really happy and really safe, one ought to have at least two or three hobbies, and they must all be real."

— SIR WINSTON CHURCHILL, _Painting As a Pastime_

www.LifeJourneyBooks.com

## Quick Quote

"Hobbies protect us from passions. One hobby becomes a passion."

— MARIE VON EBNER-ESCHENBACH

## Life-Bit

"The family legend is that Bernard Vonnegut when a boy was working with his brothers in the family hardware store, and he began to weep. He was asked what the trouble was, and he said that he didn't want to work in a store. He wanted to be an artist instead."

— KURT VONNEGUT, *Palm Sunday: An Autobiographical Collage*

**12.** **Highlight the most memorable moments in your pursuit of your passion.** Whether it's finding that rare coin, seeing your garden flourish or winning a prize for your painting, list the times that you'll never forget.

_____

_____

_____

_____

_____

_____

_____

_____

_____

_____

_____

_____

_____

_____

## Don't Forget to PLET!

**Now return to Chapter 2 to add Pivotal Life Events you remembered during this chapter. You'll be glad you did!!**

# 16 My Communal Self: The Commitments That Mattered

**1. What was your earliest organizational involvement as a child?** The Scouts? A sports team? A club? A church or synagogue youth group? Please tell us how you got involved.

LET'S EXPLORE the ways in which you have worked to make your community and the world a better place. Over the years, as you have evolved and developed, many of your allegiances and involvements – politically, religiously, civically, socially – have changed whereas others have stayed the same and even grown stronger. Together we will see how these commitments and causes have affected both your life and your world.

2. **Share the kinds of memorable activities you took part in through the early involvement you told us about on the previous page.** What was your favorite activity and why? Please provide as many details as you can recall.

_____

_____

_____

_____

_____

_____

_____

_____

_____

_____

_____

_____

_____

_____

_____

_____

_____

**3.** **As a young adult what kinds of organizational involvements defined and expressed your interests and beliefs at the time?** Please tell us how you got involved.

_____

_____

_____

_____

_____

_____

_____

_____

_____

_____

_____

_____

_____

_____

_____

_____

_____

_____

_____

_____

## Today's Tip

Can you list three adjectives that describe your role in this early organizational involvement?

## Quick Quote

"I have long recognized a link between fitness and mental health and I think we need to encourage young people to take part in sports and team activities because we know it has such positive results."

— TIPPER GORE

## Life-Bit

"… when I was a student at the Eastman School of Music, I became exposed to a lot more musical forms, elements, opportunities, and I fell in love with strings and their uses."

— CHUCK MANGIONE

www.LifeJourneyBooks.com

4. **As you grew and matured, how did your involvements and commitments develop and change?** Please provide specific examples of those involvements you left behind and those you picked up along the way.

**5.** **What area of volunteer work has proven most gratifying to you?** How did that develop? Whom did you help? Please give a few details.

_____

_____

_____

_____

_____

_____

_____

_____

_____

_____

_____

_____

_____

_____

_____

_____

_____

_____

_____

_____

Can you list the top three satisfactions of your favorite volunteer work?

## Quick Quote

"The magnitude of our social problems will require that all citizens and institutions make a commitment to volunteering as a way of life and as a primary opportunity to create needed change."

— GEORGE ROMNEY

## Life-Bit

"My parents had chosen for me the Paston School in North Walsham, Norfolk, a direct-grant grammar whose major claim to fame was having had Horatio Nelson as an unhappy pupil."

– STEPHEN FRY, *The Fry Chronicles*

6. **Did your parents' involvements and commitments influence your own?** If so, in what ways? Kindly share an example or two to illustrate.

_____

_____

_____

_____

_____

_____

_____

_____

_____

_____

_____

_____

_____

_____

_____

_____

_____

_____

**7.** **Did you get involved in community service with a friend?** A relative? Who? Why do you think you made a good team? Please give an example of something you did together with as many details as you can.

_____

_____

_____

_____

_____

_____

_____

_____

_____

_____

_____

_____

_____

_____

_____

_____

_____

_____

_____

_____

Who taught your deepest core value to you? Please name the person and the value.

"The miracle is this - the more we share, the more we have."

— LEONARD NIMOY

"Woe to him that is alone when he falls; for he has not another to help him up."

— ECCLESIASTES 9:4, *The Bible*

**8.** **Which of your organizational involvements best reflects your deepest core values and why?** Please share an example to illustrate.

_____

_____

_____

_____

_____

_____

_____

_____

_____

_____

_____

_____

_____

_____

_____

_____

_____

_____

**Just remembered something else?**
**Feel free to use your extra pages at the end of this chapter.**

## 9. If you were asked to give advice to someone looking for a cause or an organization to become involved in, what advice would you give and why?

_____

_____

_____

_____

_____

_____

_____

_____

_____

_____

_____

_____

_____

_____

_____

_____

_____

_____

_____

_____

_____

_____

Name one cause that you now regret getting involved with. Why?

"Never doubt that a small group of thoughtful, committed citizens can change the world; indeed, it's the only thing that ever has."

— MARGARET MEAD

" ... the most acceptable service we can render to Him is doing good to His other children."

— BENJAMIN FRANKLIN, *The Autobiography of Benjamin Franklin*

**10.** **In what groups and organizations do you still participate?** What keeps you involved?

_____

_____

_____

_____

_____

_____

_____

_____

_____

_____

_____

_____

_____

_____

_____

_____

_____

_____

_____

_____

## 11. What other involvements do you *wish* you'd pursued?
Why? What prevented you from getting involved at the time?

_____

_____

_____

_____

_____

_____

_____

_____

_____

_____

_____

_____

_____

_____

_____

_____

_____

_____

**12.** **Please name at least one group or cause that you still want to get involved in.** What attracts you to it?

_____

_____

_____

_____

_____

_____

_____

_____

_____

_____

_____

_____

_____

_____

_____

_____

## Don't Forget to PLET!

Now return to Chapter 2 to add Pivotal Life Events you remembered during this chapter. You'll be glad you did!!

# 17 Losses, Second Chances and Other Life Changes

**1.** **Did you experience the loss of a loved one?** Who was it? Did anything help you get through the darkest moments? Please tell us about the experience.

_____

_____

_____

_____

_____

_____

_____

_____

_____

_____

_____

_____

_____

_____

_____

_____

_____

_____

WHAT AND WHOM have you lost during your lifetime? A spouse, be it to divorce or death? Your parents or brothers or sisters? A child? A job? A home? Here we will ask you to share what you miss most, how you dealt with these losses and what - or who - pulled you through. We will also explore the often surprising new opportunities to love, as well as new homes, careers and families.

Do you have pictures and other mementos of those you have lost? Take them out and look at them before you start writing. Keep them nearby as you work your way through this chapter.

"And remember, it's also very funny, because side by side with grief lies joy."

— FRAN DRESCHER

"The only upside in this respect is at least Marlon and I were away from the immediate grief. I had to go on stage that night. After that it was plowing through the tour with Marlon and keeping that separated. It made Marlon and me tighter, no matter what. I've lost my second son. I ain't going to lose the first."

– KEITH RICHARDS, JAMES FOX, *Life*

2. **Who was there to provide support in your grief?** Please tell us in detail how they helped.

_____

_____

_____

_____

_____

_____

_____

_____

_____

_____

_____

_____

_____

_____

_____

_____

_____

_____

## 3. Do you ever talk with a loved one who's passed away?

What kinds of things do you confide in them? Does it help? If so, please describe one such encounter.

_____

_____

_____

_____

_____

_____

_____

_____

_____

_____

_____

_____

_____

_____

_____

_____

_____

_____

_____

_____

_____

_____

Scan all the old pictures you have of your loved one (or have someone do it for you) into a computer and create a DVD (someone can do this also) you will cherish.

## Quick Quote

"To live in hearts we leave behind is not to die."

—— THOMAS CAMPBELL, *Hallowed Ground*

## Life-Bit

"My grandmother decided that we children should not go to the funeral, and so I had no tangible thing to make death real to me. From that time on, I knew in my mind that my father was dead, and yet I lived with him more closely, probably, than I had when he was alive."

— ELEANOR ROOSEVELT, *The Autobiography of Eleanor Roosevelt*

4. **What things do you miss most about your loved one?**
Please give detailed examples.

_____

_____

_____

_____

_____

_____

_____

_____

_____

_____

_____

_____

_____

_____

_____

_____

_____

_____

**5.** **Share the most precious memory you have of someone you lost.** Please be sure to include as many details as you can.

_____

_____

_____

_____

_____

_____

_____

_____

_____

_____

_____

_____

_____

_____

_____

_____

_____

_____

_____

_____

_____

## Today's Tip

If you can, call someone who knew your loved one well and remember that person together.

## Quick Quote

"Unable are the loved to die. For love is immortality."

— EMILY DICKINSON

## Life-Bit

"I mourned the fact that we could not attend the free concert the remaining Stones held in his memory … culminating with Mick Jagger releasing scores of white doves into the London sky. I laid my drawing pencils aside and began a cycle of love poems to Brian Jones…"

– PATTI SMITH, _Just Kids_

Have there been particular foods that have given you comfort in hard times? If you can, make those dishes that made you feel better in your darkest hours (or ask someone else to make them).

## Quick Quote

"A man has no more character than he can command in a time of crisis."

— RALPH W. SOCKMAN

## Life-Bit

"I can see that all of life is cyclical. What is happening has happened before and will happen again. This realization makes me feel better because I know this too shall pass. We know we have to get through the night in order to have the day."

— SHIRLEY MACLAINE,
*I'm Over All That*

**6. Did you experience a loss of a job, a home, a financial setback?** Describe each one. What got you through each crisis? (Don't forget to use the extra pages whenever you need them)

**7.** **Did you get a new job?** Change careers? If so, did your new job provide you with unexpected satisfactions? Please describe.

**8. Did you make a big move?** Did you welcome the change or mourn your previous home? Describe why you moved and what it took to adjust to your new home and community. Please give enough details to illustrate your reactions.

_____

_____

_____

_____

_____

_____

_____

_____

_____

_____

_____

_____

_____

_____

**Just remembered something else?**
**Feel free to use your extra pages at the end of this chapter.**

## 9. Did you experience divorce?
What caused the breakup? Who and what got you through this crisis? Please provide as many details as you can.

_____

_____

_____

_____

_____

_____

_____

_____

_____

_____

_____

_____

_____

_____

_____

_____

_____

_____

_____

_____

_____

_____

If widowed or divorced, please describe your first date after becoming single again.

"If you have made mistakes, even serious ones, there is always another chance for you. What we call failure is not the falling down but the staying down."

— MARY PICKFORD

"I'd never before felt this ecstasy at the taste of being alive. Everything was in vivid colors now. Smells were pungent. The ordinary was extraordinary."

— ALAN ALDA, *Never Have Your Dog Stuffed*

## 10. Did you get another opportunity to love in your life?

How did it happen? (Don't skimp on the details!)

_____

_____

_____

_____

_____

_____

_____

_____

_____

_____

_____

_____

_____

_____

_____

_____

_____

_____

## 11. If remarried, did it involve children, grandchildren? How did they react to the new family arrangement? How did you? How did your new spouse? Please tell us about it in detail!

_____

_____

_____

_____

_____

_____

_____

_____

_____

_____

_____

_____

_____

_____

_____

_____

_____

_____

_____

_____

12. **Second marriages and new jobs present opportunities for many new relationships – from new colleagues to a new sister-in-law to a new stepchild.** Describe some of the closest relationships that evolved from these "second chances" in your life.

_____

_____

_____

_____

_____

_____

_____

_____

_____

_____

_____

_____

_____

_____

_____

_____

## Don't Forget to PLET!

Now return to Chapter 2 to add Pivotal Life Events you remembered during this chapter. You'll be glad you did!!

## 18 More Kids to Love: Becoming a Grandparent

**1.** **What was your reaction when you first learned you were going to be a grandparent?** Please tell us the whole story and don't skimp on the details!

_____

_____

_____

_____

_____

_____

_____

_____

_____

_____

_____

_____

_____

_____

_____

_____

_____

_____

_____

_____

_____

HERE WE INVITE you to delve into the satisfactions and joys, the highs and even the occasional lows, of your role as grandparent. We will ask you to tell us about each special grandchild - and any great-grandchildren you may be blessed with – along with your hopes and dreams for them. How do they remind you of your younger self or your spouse, even as they grow up in such a different world? Note: If you don't have grandchildren, please answer the following questions for beloved grand-nieces, grand-nephews or godchildren.

What name do the grandkids call you? Please think back on how you got that name and tell us all about it.

## Quick Quote

"Grandchildren are God's way of compensating us for growing old."

— MARY H. WALDRIP

## Life-Bit

"The pattern has shifted; we have changed places in the dance. I am no longer anybody's child. I have become the Grandmother. It is going to take a while to get used to this unfamiliar role."

— MADELEINE L'ENGLE, *The Summer of the Great-grandmother*

2. **Please describe the first time you met your first grandchild, including the details and your thoughts and feelings that day.**

_____

_____

_____

_____

_____

_____

_____

_____

_____

_____

_____

_____

_____

_____

_____

_____

_____

_____

_____

**3.** **Please list all your grandchildren (and great-grandchildren if you have them) including their birth dates, along with one telling experience with each of them.** You can use the extra pages provided and go into as much detail as possible!

_____

_____

_____

_____

_____

_____

_____

_____

_____

_____

_____

_____

_____

_____

_____

_____

_____

_____

_____

## Today's Tip

Please sketch the layout of the room where you met your first grandchild for the first time. Where was it? Don't forget to mark the spot where you and the baby were.

## Quick Quote

"Grandchildren don't make a man feel old; it's the knowledge that he's married to a grandmother."

— G. NORMAN COLLIE

## Life-Bit

"When the news came that Sevanne Margaret was born, I suddenly realized that, through no act of my own, I had become biologically related to a new human being ... In the presence of grandparent and grandchild, past and future merge in the present."

— MARGARET MEAD,
_Blackberry Winter:
My Earlier Years_

Please name one way that one of your grandchildren reminds you of yourself at their age and please include their name and age.

*"The idea that no one is perfect is a view most commonly held by people with no grandchildren."*

— DOUG LARSON

"'Are you special, Grandpa?' she asked. 'No more or less than anyone else,' I said. 'Can I be like that someday?' she asked. 'You already are,' I said."

— DICK VAN DYKE, *My Lucky Life In and Out of Show Business*

4. **How do you relate differently to your grandchildren than you did to your own children?** Please give examples to illustrate the differences.

_____

_____

_____

_____

_____

_____

_____

_____

_____

_____

_____

_____

_____

_____

_____

_____

_____

**5.** **How did your grandchildren change your relationship with your children?** Please give an example or two ... or three.

_____

_____

_____

_____

_____

_____

_____

_____

_____

_____

_____

_____

_____

_____

_____

_____

_____

_____

## Today's Tip

Close your eyes and travel back over the years. Now ask yourself approximately what percentage of the time did you say "no" to your children. Now write down approximately what percentage of the time you say "no" to your grandchildren (or great-grandchildren)!

## Quick Quote

"When grandparents enter the door, discipline flies out the window."

— OGDEN NASH

## Life-Bit

"My granddaughter Ty is very interested in learning to make my chickweed salve. It'll heal about anything."

— AMY HILL HEARTH, _Strong Medicine Speaks: A Native American Elder Has Her Say_

Please tell us: If you could teach one thing to your children about parenting, what would it be?

"The best babysitters, of course, are the baby's grandparents. You feel completely comfortable entrusting your baby to them for long periods, which is why most grandparents flee to Florida."

— DAVE BARRY

"It was sheer joy watching my daughter feel the same feelings I had when she was growing inside me. I loved every moment of sharing all the physical and emotional changes in Kate, of being able to identify so closely with the experience and compare it with my own."

— GOLDIE HAWN,
*A Lotus Grows in the Mud*

**6. Please describe in detail a particularly joyful moment of grandparenting.** Don't spare the details!

_____

_____

_____

_____

_____

_____

_____

_____

_____

_____

_____

_____

_____

_____

_____

_____

_____

_____

## 7. Please describe in detail a particularly *difficult* moment of grandparenting.

_____

_____

_____

_____

_____

_____

_____

_____

_____

_____

_____

_____

_____

_____

_____

_____

_____

_____

_____

_____

_____

_____

_____

### Today's Tip

In 50 words or less, please share your personal secret of successful grandparenting.

### Quick Quote

"Few things are more satisfying than seeing your children have teenagers of their own."

— DOUG LARSON

### Life-Bit

"All who saw my grandson Benny agreed of his being an uncommonly fine boy."

— BENJAMIN FRANKLIN, *The Autobiography of Benjamin Franklin*

If you could change one thing for your grandchildren, what would it be?

"Tough times never last but tough people do."

— ROBERT SCHULLER

"He (my grandson) was looking well and happy, with a crinkled-up face and a slight grin which was probably wind but looked like amiability."

— AGATHA CHRISTIE,
*Agatha Christie:
An Autobiography*

**8.** **How does the world your grandchildren live in differ from the one you raised your children in?** Please give examples.

_____

_____

_____

_____

_____

_____

_____

_____

_____

_____

_____

_____

_____

_____

_____

_____

_____

**Just remembered something else?**
**Feel free to use your extra pages at the end of this chapter.**

## 9. What are your highest hopes for your grandchildren?
Please give examples.

_____

_____

_____

_____

_____

_____

_____

_____

_____

_____

_____

_____

_____

_____

_____

_____

_____

_____

_____

_____

_____

_____

_____

Name one major advantage your grandchildren have that you did not.

"Nobody can do for little children what grandparents do. Grandparents sort of sprinkle stardust over the lives of little children."

— ALEX HALEY

"(My grandson) Nathan has always been ahead of himself, acting older than his age … more like a twenty-five year old than a sixteen year old. He says he wants to carry the music forward … I'm all for him … he's a lot further advanced than we are."

— DR. RALPH STANLEY, *Man of Constant Sorrow*

## 10. What are your greatest fears for your grandchildren?
Please give examples of these too.

_____

_____

_____

_____

_____

_____

_____

_____

_____

_____

_____

_____

_____

_____

_____

_____

_____

_____

## 11. What's the most important piece of advice you would like to give your grandchildren today? Why?

_____

_____

_____

_____

_____

_____

_____

_____

_____

_____

_____

_____

_____

_____

_____

_____

_____

_____

_____

_____

Do you remember a piece of parenting advice your own grandparent (or other older relative) gave you? Please share it with us.

"If becoming a grandmother was only a matter of choice, I should advise every one of you straight away to become one. There is no fun for old people like it!"

— HANNAH WHITHALL SMITH

"'Taylor, you will have to do all the birthdays you've had in your life eight times to be as old as Poppy,' I say. She'll think for a minute and then say something like, 'But I haven't had my birthday this year and I want a cookies 'n' cream ice cream cake.'"

– BOB NEWHART, *I Shouldn't Even Be Doing This: And Other Things That Strike Me as Funny*

## 12. How has becoming a grandparent – or godparent, great aunt or uncle – changed you and the way you view the world?

Please be as specific as possible!

_____

_____

_____

_____

_____

_____

_____

_____

_____

_____

_____

_____

_____

_____

_____

_____

_____

_____

**Don't Forget to PLET!**

Now return to Chapter 2 to add Pivotal Life Events you remembered during this chapter. You'll be glad you did!!

# 19 Leaving the Grind Behind: The Retirement Years

**1. How did you envision retirement when you were still working?** Please provide specific details! Did reality match the vision ... or not? Please give a few examples.

_____

_____

_____

_____

_____

_____

_____

_____

_____

_____

_____

_____

_____

_____

_____

_____

_____

_____

_____

_____

SOME OF US walk away from our jobs with a laugh, others with a tear. But for most of us it's a combination of joy and sorrow, celebration and regret, anticipation and loss. Here's your chance to truly discover the role that the final days of your career - and the leaving it behind - has played in your life journey. Note: If you didn't work, please answer the questions as your spouse's career affected *your* life.

"Retirement is not a time to sleep, but a time to awaken to the beauty of the world around you and the joy that comes when you cast out all the negative elements that cause confusion and turmoil in your mind and allow serenity to prevail."

— HOWARD SALZMAN

"Every day I asked myself, wondering aloud, 'What does the future hold for you now, Goldie Hawn?' The best thing of all is I just don't know."

— GOLDIE HAWN,
*A Lotus Grows in the Mud*

2. **Why did you retire?** Was it your decision or not? Did you feel ready to retire at the time? Please describe the circumstances.

_____

_____

_____

_____

_____

_____

_____

_____

_____

_____

_____

_____

_____

_____

_____

_____

_____

_____

3. **How old were you when you retired?** Where were you living? How did retiring change your life? What was the biggest adjustment you had to make? Please give details.

_____

_____

_____

_____

_____

_____

_____

_____

_____

_____

_____

_____

_____

_____

_____

_____

_____

_____

_____

## Quick Quote

"I've been working in show
business for eighty-six years,
if this keeps up maybe I
should consider making it
my career."

— GEORGE BURNS

## Life-Bit

"As my children were finding
themselves, I was going
through the same thing, a
sort of adult-onset confusion
that had me asking many of
the same questions: What
was I going to do with my
life? What was going to
make me happy? Why wasn't
I happy?"

— DICK VAN DYKE,
*My Lucky Life In and
Out of Show Business*

4. **What did you miss most about the working life?**
Please give concrete examples.

_____

_____

_____

_____

_____

_____

_____

_____

_____

_____

_____

_____

_____

_____

_____

_____

_____

_____

## 5. What aspects of working were you glad to put behind you?
Please give specifics.

_____

_____

_____

_____

_____

_____

_____

_____

_____

_____

_____

_____

_____

_____

_____

_____

_____

_____

_____

_____

_____

_____

Describe what parts of your job used to make a work day feel particularly long.

"I love my past. I love my present. I'm not ashamed of what I've had, and I'm not sad because I have it no longer."

— COLLETTE

"Slowly, slowly we began to rise ... the White House was behind us now .... There was no talk. There were no tears left."

— RICHARD NIXON, *The Memoirs of Richard Nixon*

6. **How have your retirement years lived up to your expectations?** How has reality been different than what you had envisioned? Please give specific examples.

_____

_____

_____

_____

_____

_____

_____

_____

_____

_____

_____

_____

_____

_____

_____

_____

_____

_____

_____

## 7. What are your current activities? Please describe a typical day in the year following your – or your spouse's – retirement.

_____

_____

_____

_____

_____

_____

_____

_____

_____

_____

_____

_____

_____

_____

_____

_____

_____

_____

_____

_____

_____

_____

## Quick Quote

"Twenty years from now you will be more disappointed by the things you didn't do than by the ones you did do. So throw off the bowlines. Sail away from the safe harbor. Catch the trade winds in your sails. Explore. Dream. Discover."

— MARK TWAIN

## Life-Bit

"Even at my present age, somewhat past puberty, my doctors tell me I don't react like a normal, grown-up person ... whatever the reason, I don't seem to get tired the way most people around me do. Time is my friend, not my enemy."

— BOB HOPE,
*Don't Shoot, It's Only Me*

**8. What are the activities you most enjoy now that you are retired?** Please describe them.

_____

_____

_____

_____

_____

_____

_____

_____

_____

_____

_____

_____

_____

_____

_____

_____

_____

**Just remembered something else?**
**Feel free to use your extra pages at the end of this chapter.**

## 9. What new skills and interests have you acquired? Did you plan on this? Please be specific.

_____

_____

_____

_____

_____

_____

_____

_____

_____

_____

_____

_____

_____

_____

_____

_____

_____

_____

_____

_____

Name one thing you never dreamed you'd ever do but that you *are* doing (or have done) in retirement.

"There's no retirement for an artist, it's your way of living so there's no end to it. "

— HENRY MOORE

"I *never* finish a day and think I'm all caught up."

— BETTY WHITE,
*If You Ask Me*

**10. Who are your favorite companions in retirement?** What interests do you share? Please describe what you do together.

_____

_____

_____

_____

_____

_____

_____

_____

_____

_____

_____

_____

_____

_____

_____

_____

_____

_____

_____

_____

_____

**11.** **How have you grown in surprising ways in your retirement years?** Please describe.

_____

_____

_____

_____

_____

_____

_____

_____

_____

_____

_____

_____

_____

_____

_____

_____

_____

_____

_____

_____

## Today's Tip

Name one personality trait that's new to you at this stage in your life.

## Quick Quote

"The older I get, the greater power I seem to have to help the world; I am like a snowball - the further I am rolled the more I gain."

— SUSAN B. ANTHONY

## Life-Bit

"No more office. No more pissed-off people on the phone. Just me and a truck and my traps and my tent. That's how I wanted it. Like the old days."

— CARTER NIEMEYER,
*Wolfer: A Memoir*

## 12. How has retirement changed your views on what's important in your life? Please tell us about it.

_____

_____

_____

_____

_____

_____

_____

_____

_____

_____

_____

_____

_____

_____

_____

_____

## Don't Forget to PLET!

Now return to Chapter 2 to add Pivotal Life Events you remembered during this chapter. You'll be glad you did!!

**1.** **Where are you living now?** Who are you living with? Please describe. Does this living arrangement suit you? Please tell us why or why not.

_____

_____

_____

_____

_____

_____

_____

_____

_____

_____

_____

_____

_____

_____

_____

_____

_____

YOUR LIFE NOW might be completely different than you ever anticipated – or exactly what you expected. Either way, it may well be filled with friends, family and activities. You could be spending your days volunteering or watching the grandkids or traveling or scrapbooking – and finally getting around to enjoying the freedom you never had before. You could also be facing new challenges, whether it's a health issue, family changes or a forced move. Here's your chance to record it all.

Make a sketch of the layout of your current home. Place all your furnishings in their correct place and don't worry if the proportions are a little off.

## Quick Quote

"I do not want people to be very agreeable, as it saves me the trouble of liking them a great deal."

— JANE AUSTEN

## Life-Bit

"This is why we older people should have dogs. It helps us go into hyperlove, and love is what ageing is all about. It is time to do away with self-deception, ambition, judgment, pettiness and self-consciousness."

– SHIRLEY MACLAINE,
*Sag-ing While Age-ing*

2. **What people - siblings, spouse, partner, children, grandchildren or friends - fill your days?** How have your relationships with them changed? Do you have a pet now? If so, tell us how s/he affects your life.

_____

_____

_____

_____

_____

_____

_____

_____

_____

_____

_____

_____

_____

_____

_____

_____

_____

## 3. Are you still in touch with your old friends? Have you made new ones? Describe your relationships with friends both old and new.

_____

_____

_____

_____

_____

_____

_____

_____

_____

_____

_____

_____

_____

_____

_____

_____

_____

_____

_____

_____

Jot down the name of the person who is still in your life and knows you best -- and not just at the age you are now.

## Quick Quote

"Don't you stay at home of evenings? Don't you love a cushioned seat in a corner, by the fireside, with your slippers on your feet?"

— OLIVER WENDELL HOLMES, SR.

## Life-Bit

"I tell myself if I win this match, I'll retire. And if I lose this match, I'll retire. I lose. I don't retire. Instead, I do the opposite of retiring: I get on a plane to Australia to play in a slam."

— ANDRE AGASSI, *Open: An Autobiography*

4. **Describe a typical day in your life now.** Start with your morning routine and take us all the way till bedtime. Please provide the details.

_____

_____

_____

_____

_____

_____

_____

_____

_____

_____

_____

_____

_____

_____

_____

_____

_____

_____

## 5. What are your most enjoyable activities these days? Which ones do you dread? Please describe them all.

_____

_____

_____

_____

_____

_____

_____

_____

_____

_____

_____

_____

_____

_____

_____

_____

_____

_____

_____

_____

_____

## Today's Tip

Please write down the name of the tune you hum most often these days. Do you tend to "hear" old favorites in your head or current popular songs?

## Quick Quote:

"The only routine with me is no routine at all."

— JACQUELINE KENNEDY ONASSIS

## Life-Bit:

"My art, work, family and friends, my son Gabe, and a curious relationship with God remain the sustaining forces of my life."

— JOAN BAEZ,
*And a Voice to Sing With: A Memoir*

## Quick Quote:

"My life is an indivisible whole, and all my activities run into one another and they have their rise in my insatiable love of mankind."

— MAHATMA GHANDI

## Life-Bit

"My greatest regret: That I never learned to play the piano. I think that if I could have learned to play the piano, practicing would have permitted me to reflect and imagine and drift and think and develop."

— ERROL FLYNN,
*My Wicked, Wicked Ways:
The Autobiography
of Errol Flynn*

6. **What do you allow yourself now for the first time that you never did before?** Please give as many details as possible.

_____

_____

_____

_____

_____

_____

_____

_____

_____

_____

_____

_____

_____

_____

_____

_____

_____

_____

_____

**7. How is your life different than it was ten years ago?** Please describe both times in terms of activities, living arrangements, responsibilities, joys and frustrations.

_____

_____

_____

_____

_____

_____

_____

_____

_____

_____

_____

_____

_____

_____

_____

_____

_____

## Quick Quote:

"The follies which a man regrets most in his life are those which he didn't commit when he had the opportunity."

— HELEN ROWLAND

## Life-Bit

"I was his sister. Who else had been there from the beginning, who else understood without saying, who would laugh at any joke, who would read the day's obituaries with him looking for friends of our parents who had at last bit the dust?"

— ANNE ROIPHE,
*1185 Park Avenue*

**8.** **Have you recently lost anyone close to you?** How has that changed your life? Please tell us about it.

_____

_____

_____

_____

_____

_____

_____

_____

_____

_____

_____

_____

_____

_____

_____

_____

_____

**Just remembered something else?**
**Feel free to use your extra pages at the end of this chapter.**

**9.** **How is your life similar or different from your parents during their senior years?** Please describe both in detail.

_____

_____

_____

_____

_____

_____

_____

_____

_____

_____

_____

_____

_____

_____

_____

_____

_____

_____

_____

_____

_____

## Today's Tip

What's your favorite piece of scripture or inspirational poem? Please write down as much as you can recall (or look up the words to refresh your memory!)

## Quick Quote

"The spiritual life does not remove us from the world but leads us deeper into it."

— HENRI J. M. NOUWEN

## Life-Bit

"If I was going to look for meaning, I didn't want meaning that would betray other people, and I also didn't want it to betray me. I wanted it to last."

— ALAN ALDA,
*Things I Overheard While Talking To Myself*

**10.** **What is your spiritual life like now?** Does it define your life more – or less – than when you were younger? Please describe your current spiritual or religious beliefs and practices.

_____

_____

_____

_____

_____

_____

_____

_____

_____

_____

_____

_____

_____

_____

_____

_____

_____

_____

**11.** **From your experience, what advice would you give to someone close to you, such as a child or niece or nephew, who is entering their senior years?** Please be as specific as possible.

_____

_____

_____

_____

_____

_____

_____

_____

_____

_____

_____

_____

_____

_____

_____

_____

_____

_____

_____

If you could go on a trip tomorrow, where would you go? What do you still yearn to experience?

"Not only is another world possible, she is on her way. On a quiet day, I can hear her breathing."

— ARUNDHATI ROY

"It's dangerous when you are older to start living in the past. Now that it's out of my system, I intend to live in the present, looking forward to the future."

— KATHARINE GRAHAM, *Personal History*

## 12. What are you looking forward to most? Feel free to go to town with the details!

_____

_____

_____

_____

_____

_____

_____

_____

_____

_____

_____

_____

_____

_____

_____

_____

_____

### Don't Forget to PLET!

**Now return to Chapter 2 to add Pivotal Life Events you remembered during this chapter. You'll be glad you did!!**

# 21 My Family Tree

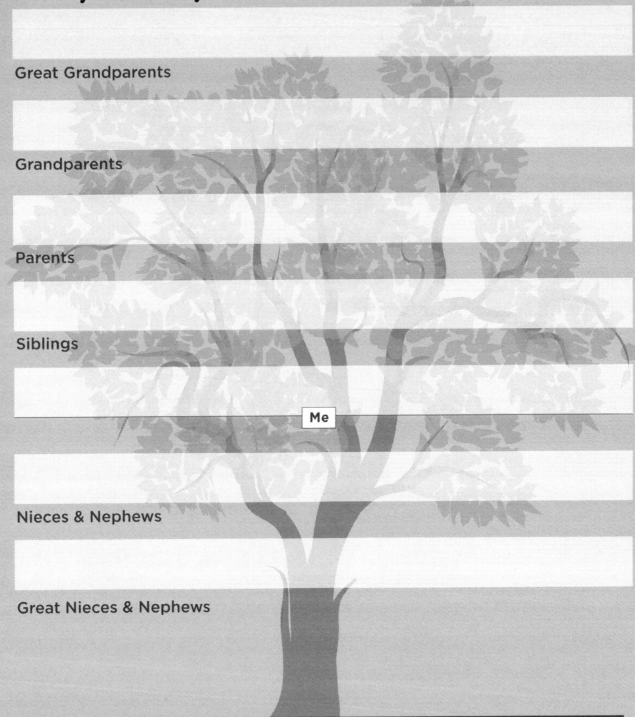

Great Grandparents

Grandparents

Parents

Siblings

Me

Nieces & Nephews

Great Nieces & Nephews

## My Family Tree
### (the family that created me)

*Please fill in the names and birth dates of you and your relatives in the spaces provided. Please include dates of death, where appropriate.*

LIFEJOURNEY BOOKS

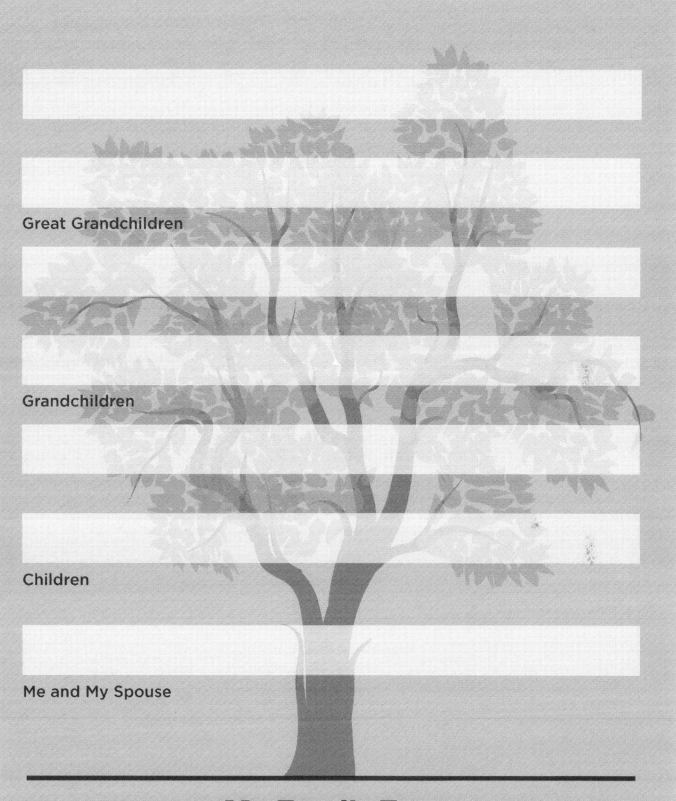

Great Grandchildren

Grandchildren

Children

Me and My Spouse

# My Family Tree
(the family that I created)

*Please fill in the names and birth dates of you and your immediate family in the spaces provided. Please include dates of death, where appropriate.*

# 22

# Where I Come From: My Family History

**1.** **Where did your mother's mother's family come from?**
What else do you know about them (languages spoken, etc.)?

_____

_____

_____

_____

_____

_____

_____

_____

_____

_____

_____

_____

_____

_____

_____

_____

_____

_____

I N SO MANY WAYS we _are_ the families we come from. So much has been passed on to us that when we think about it, we can identify much of ourselves in the genetic mix. And a lot of it – but not all! – we hope to transmit to those who come after. The focus here is on what we inherited and how we are passing that along to future generations. Here's where we explore family origins, including immigrations, surnames and even talents and family quirks that may have skipped a generation or two.

2. **Where did your mother's father's family come from?** What do you know about them (languages spoken, etc.)?

_____

_____

_____

_____

_____

_____

_____

_____

_____

_____

_____

_____

_____

_____

_____

_____

_____

_____

_____

## 3. Where did your father's mother's family come from? What do you know about them (languages spoken, etc.)?

_____

_____

_____

_____

_____

_____

_____

_____

_____

_____

_____

_____

_____

_____

_____

_____

_____

_____

_____

_____

### Today's Tip

If your mother's family had a creed or slogan what would it be?

### Quick Quote

"One faces the future with one's past."

— PEARL BUCK

### Life-Bit

"… I did not want to be the next edition of Billy Hamill … if there were patterns, endless repetitions, cycles of family history, if my father was the result of his father and his father's father, on back through the generation of the Irish fogs, I could no longer accept any notion of predestination. Someone among the males of this family had to break the pattern. It might as well be me. I didn't have a drink."

— PETE HAMILL,
_A Drinking Life_

If your father's family had a creed or slogan what would it be?

"My father, an enlightened spirit, believed in man. My grandfather, a fervent Hasid, believed in G-d. The one taught me to speak, the other to sing. Both loved stories. And when I tell mine, I hear their voices. Whispering from beyond the silenced storm. They are what links the survivor to their memory."

— ELIE WIESEL

"I cannot think of any need in childhood as strong as the need for a father's protection."

—SIGMUND FREUD

## 4. Where did your father's father's family come from?

What do you know about them (languages spoken, etc.)?

**5.** **In what ways do you physically resemble your mother's or father's family?** Can you identify which of your forbearers certain features came down from? Please describe them as accurately as possible.

_____
_____
_____
_____
_____
_____
_____
_____
_____
_____
_____
_____
_____
_____
_____
_____
_____
_____
_____

Do you ever hear a parent's "voice" in your head when trying to make a decision? What does she or he tell you to do? Do you typically follow their advice?

## Quick Quote

"I suppose it is inescapable that for a long time we know our parents only as parents, that their separate identity as full persons in their own right unfolds only gradually, if at all."

— MADELEINE L'ENGLE

## Life-Bit

"Your parents, they give you your life, but then they try to give you their life."

— CHUCK PALAHNIUK, *Invisible Monsters*

**6.** **Which of your values and the decisions you have made reflect qualities of your parents and grandparents?** Whom do you think they came from? Please describe.

_____

_____

_____

_____

_____

_____

_____

_____

_____

_____

_____

_____

_____

_____

_____

_____

_____

_____

_____

_____

**7.** **Which of your children and/or grandchildren (or, if you don't have children, which of your nieces or nephews) have inherited physical or character traits or talents from your family?** Tell us a bit about these and where you think they came from.

_____

_____

_____

_____

_____

_____

_____

_____

_____

_____

_____

_____

_____

_____

_____

_____

_____

_____

## Today's Tip:

Time to haul out those photos (and reading glasses) again! Please write down which of the younger generation closely resembles your family. Please tell us who and describe in what way.

## Quick Quote

"Heredity is what sets the parents of a teenager wondering about each other."

— LAURENCE J. PETER

## Life-Bit

"When I was a boy of fourteen, my father was so ignorant I could hardly stand to have the old man around. But when I got to be twenty-one, I was astonished at how much he had learned in seven years."

— MARK TWAIN, _Old Times On The Mississippi_

www.LifeJourneyBooks.com

Which of the younger generation has the personality traits most like your family? Who do you think he or she got them from? How do you predict these qualities will help or challenge them in life?

## Quick Quote

"That's sort of a cliché about parents. We all believe that our children are the most beautiful children in the world. But the thing is, what no one really talks about is the fact that we all really believe it."

—HEATHER ARMSTRONG

## Life-Bit

"My mother was the daughter of a strict Baptist matriarch who barred dancing, dating and card-playing, and she must have viewed her marriage to my theatrically inclined father as an exciting alternative to small town life. But my father overpowered her easily intimidated personality, and she only escaped from one repressive situation into another."

—STEVE MARTIN, *Born Standing Up: A Comic's Life*

**8.** **Which character traits and values from your family do you hope your children and/or grandchildren (or, if you don't have children, which of your nieces or nephews) and future generations inherit?** Where and with whom do you think these traits originated?

_____

_____

_____

_____

_____

_____

_____

_____

_____

_____

_____

_____

_____

_____

**Just remembered something else?**
**Feel free to use your extra pages at the end of this chapter.**

**9.** **Which of your accomplishments do you believe your parents, grandparents and, if possible, great-grandparents would be the most proud of?** Please tell us how these forbearers and in some detail how they exemplified those values themselves.

_____

_____

_____

_____

_____

_____

_____

_____

_____

_____

_____

_____

_____

_____

_____

_____

_____

_____

_____

_____

**Quick Quote**

"The older I get, the more I think about God, the more about my life's meaning…"

— SHIRLEY MACLAINE

**Life-Bit**

"It is quite easy for me to think of a God of love mainly because I grew up in a family where love was central and where loving relationships were ever present … It is quite easy for me to lean more toward optimism than pessimism about human nature mainly because of my childhood experiences."

— MARTIN LUTHER KING, JR., *The Autobiography of Martin Luther King, Jr.*

10. **What religion were your parents and grandparents born into, and your family as far back as you can trace it?** Please share two or three of the oldest religious traditions of your family and tell us a bit about where they originated.

_____

_____

_____

_____

_____

_____

_____

_____

_____

_____

_____

_____

_____

_____

_____

_____

**11.** **What are the last names of your family (Please list the ones of all four grandparents).** Please share what you know about where these derived from, their meanings or other bits of their history and background.

_____

_____

_____

_____

_____

_____

_____

_____

_____

_____

_____

_____

_____

_____

_____

_____

_____

_____

_____

_____

## Today's Tip

Which of the new generation of your family bears the last name you were born with and which bears your married last name (where applicable)? What legacies do you hope (or fear!) these names carry with them?

## Quick Quote

"I used to think freedom means doing whatever you want. It means knowing who you are, what you are supposed to be doing on this earth … recording your family's history before it all passes and is gone."

— NATALIE GOLDBERG

## Life-Bit

"Hearing my name, I flung myself into the pool, hitting the water in an ungraceful belly flop, and came up gasping and thrashing … I struggled out of the pool and heard something absolutely delicious from the crowd – applause and cheers."

— ESTHER WILLIAMS, _The Million Dollar Mermaid_

Please fill in these blanks (being as honest as you can): The quality I inherited that has been the biggest help has been ---------------. The quality I inherited that has been the biggest hindrance has been-----.

## Quick Quote

"If you cannot get rid of the family skeleton, make it dance!"

— GEORGE BERNARD SHAW

## Life-Bit

"What I can certainly see is that our family were people of good will but with a disastrous heritage of guilty conscience and too great demands made on them."

— INGMAR BERGMAN, *The Magic Lantern: An Autobiography*

**12. What's an unusual quality about your family?** How does that quality express itself in previous and current generations? Please give enough details to illustrate.

_____

_____

_____

_____

_____

_____

_____

_____

_____

_____

_____

_____

_____

_____

_____

_____

_____

_____

## Don't Forget to PLET!

Now return to Chapter 2 to add Pivotal Life Events you remembered during this chapter. You'll be glad you did!!

# 23

# Who Am I? My Answers to Life's Big Questions

**1.** **What was the most powerful force that shaped your character?** Whether it's an event or sudden change in circumstances or the influence of a family member, teacher, clergyperson or someone else, please tell us about it and its impact on who you would become.

HERE IT IS: WHAT truly matters. What you have spent a lifetime honing in on, wrestling with, refining and learning. By now, we've reached the place in our work together where you're ready to tackle some of these fundamental, core questions about your life. Please give yourself the time to think these through before writing down even one word. It's often helpful to talk them over, if possible with someone who has known you for a long time. Please remember: Some of these questions might give you a moment's pause, whereas others will require some serious soul-searching. We recommend you start with a rough draft on scrap paper or the computer. If it takes a few revisions before you're ready to record your final answer, we consider that the ultimate success. Because it's never too late to get to know your true self and what's important to you … in fact it's one of the greatest joys of the LifeStorytelling journey!

Fill in the blank with the first words that come to mind: (Don't overthink this one!) I am even more _____ than I am _____ but I am even more _____ than I am _____.

## Quick Quote

"Sooner or later we all discover that the important moments in life are not the advertised ones, not the birthdays, the graduations, the weddings, not the great goals achieved. The real milestones are less prepossessing. They come to the door of memory unannounced, stray dogs that amble in, sniff around a bit and simply never leave. Our lives are measured by these."

— SUSAN B. ANTHONY

## Life-Bit

"After my father died, I came to realize something that I'm sure everyone who has ever lost someone they loved has learned. And it is – love endures … It doesn't diminish. It doesn't divert. It endures, intact."

— MARLO THOMAS, *Growing Up Laughing*

2. **What was your greatest advantage growing up as you did?**
Did you use it wisely? Why or why not?

_____

_____

_____

_____

_____

_____

_____

_____

_____

_____

_____

_____

_____

_____

_____

_____

_____

_____

_____

**3. What was your greatest disadvantage growing up?** How did you deal with it? Are you proud of that? Why or why not?

_____

_____

_____

_____

_____

_____

_____

_____

_____

_____

_____

_____

_____

_____

_____

_____

_____

_____

_____

_____

Please fill in the blank: I have been a hero to -------.

"Life, misfortunes, isolation, abandonment, poverty, are battlefields which have their heroes; obscure heroes, sometimes, greater than the illustrious heroes."

— VICTOR HUGO

"Some of us hear the singing of angels, harmonies in a heavenly choir, or at least the music of the spheres."

— MAYA ANGELOU,
*A Song Flung Up to Heaven*

4. **Who is your hero or heroine?** What were their qualities that made you select that person?

_____

_____

_____

_____

_____

_____

_____

_____

_____

_____

_____

_____

_____

_____

_____

_____

_____

_____

_____

**5. What has been your worst fear?** When did you feel it most intensely? How did you cope with it? Please provide at least one example of how your coping mechanism has worked.

_____

_____

_____

_____

_____

_____

_____

_____

_____

_____

_____

_____

_____

_____

_____

_____

_____

_____

Please fill in the blank: If there's one thing I could turn the clock back about and do over, it would be ------------ --------.

"I went out onto the balcony and stood there for a long time contemplating the heavenly bodies. I asked them mutely, 'What do you say to all this?' And I imagined that they replied, 'We have seen it all before.'"

— ISAAC BASHEVIS SINGER

"I would rather die on the highways of Alabama than make a butchery of my conscience."

— MARTIN LUTHER KING, JR., *The Autobiography of Martin Luther King, Jr.*

**6. What is the most positive change in the world in your lifetime?** The most negative change? Please give specific details with these observations.

_____

_____

_____

_____

_____

_____

_____

_____

_____

_____

_____

_____

_____

_____

_____

_____

_____

_____

_____

**7. What is the biggest blessing you have been given?** Why do you think you received it? How has it changed your life?

_____

_____

_____

_____

_____

_____

_____

_____

_____

_____

_____

_____

_____

_____

_____

_____

_____

_____

_____

Close your eyes and ask yourself to finish this sentence: A song that always makes me feel sad is --------- -------

"Life is full of misery, loneliness, and suffering - and it's all over much too soon."

— WOODY ALLEN

"It is startling to realize that one is so deeply, fanatically disliked by a number of people ... when I believe, after weighing the evidence, that what I am doing is right, I go ahead and try as hard as I can to dismiss from my mind the attitude of those who are hostile, I don't see how else one can live."

— ELEANOR ROOSEVELT, *The Autobiography of Eleanor Roosevelt*

**8.** **What is the biggest challenge you have faced?** How have you dealt with it? Please give details. Are you proud of that? Why or why not?

_____

_____

_____

_____

_____

_____

_____

_____

_____

_____

_____

_____

_____

_____

_____

_____

**Just remembered something else?**
**Feel free to use your extra pages at the end of this chapter.**

### 9. What is the most important lesson you have learned along the way? How did you learn it and how has it changed your life?

_____

_____

_____

_____

_____

_____

_____

_____

_____

_____

_____

_____

_____

_____

_____

_____

_____

_____

_____

_____

_____

Ask yourself: If you could receive one trophy for your entire life, what would be engraved on it?

"The world remembers me as a movie star, but most of my life I have thought of myself in various family roles – as daughter, sister, wife and, above all, mother."

— ESTHER WILLIAMS

"It's going to be a really big show."

— ED SULLIVAN

**10. What is your greatest achievement, the thing you're most proud of in your life?** Please describe.

_____

_____

_____

_____

_____

_____

_____

_____

_____

_____

_____

_____

_____

_____

_____

_____

_____

_____

_____

_____

## 11. When have you most strongly felt a spiritual presence in your life? Please describe the setting and situation.

_____

_____

_____

_____

_____

_____

_____

_____

_____

_____

_____

_____

_____

_____

_____

_____

_____

_____

_____

Please list each of the following: Your father's guiding principle, your mother's guiding principle and, where applicable, your spouse's guiding principle.

## Quick Quote

"You should live until you die."

— ELISABETH KUBLER-ROSS

## Life-Bit

"I believe it was from his faith in people that he drew the words for his first inaugural address: The only thing we have to fear is fear itself."

— ELEANOR ROOSEVELT, *The Autobiography of Eleanor Roosevelt*

## 12. If there is one guiding principle you have lived by, what is it? How has it influenced your life experiences?

_____

_____

_____

_____

_____

_____

_____

_____

_____

_____

_____

_____

_____

_____

_____

_____

## Don't Forget to PLET!

Now return to Chapter 2 to add Pivotal Life Events you remembered during this chapter. You'll be glad you did!!

# 24 My Enduring Principles: An Ethical Will Questionnaire

**1. Looking at your past, what were the greatest influences that shaped your principles and beliefs?** Please tell us about them in as much detail as you can.

_____

_____

_____

_____

_____

_____

_____

_____

_____

_____

_____

_____

_____

_____

_____

_____

_____

_____

_____

B Y COMPLETING this worksheet and answering these questions you will quickly identify the core values that continue to guide you and which you are committed to preserving and passing on to your children, grandchildren, other loved ones and future generations. In addition, these answers will elicit information about your beloved charities and causes you've supported financially and with your time. Now, as you are able to convey your long-held commitments, it should inspire your loved ones to follow in your footsteps.

Before you answer these questions, it will be helpful to refer back to your PLET (Pivotal Life Events Timeline) in Chapter 2 to review those events (some momentous and others that seemed minor at the time) that changed your life forever.

## Quick Quote

"Experience is the name everyone gives to their mistakes."

— OSCAR WILDE

## Life-Bit

"I did learn a lesson from that whole experience: If you make the wrong decision, it's never too late to make the right one."

— MICHAEL OHER, DON YAEGE, *I Beat the Odds: From Homelessness, to the Blind Side, and Beyond*

2. **Looking back, what was your most powerful, life-shaping experience to date?** How did it change you? Please give as many specifics as you can.

_____

_____

_____

_____

_____

_____

_____

_____

_____

_____

_____

_____

_____

_____

_____

_____

_____

_____

$3.$ **What are the strongest principles you stand for?** Please be specific.

_____
_____
_____
_____
_____
_____
_____
_____
_____
_____
_____
_____
_____
_____
_____
_____
_____
_____
_____
_____
_____

Name one thing you might have done differently if you didn't have your core values.

"Those are my principles, and if you don't like them ... well, I have others."

— GROUCHO MARX

"Democracy triumphed in the cold war because it was a battle of values – between one system that gave preeminence to the state and another that gave preeminence to the individual and freedom."

— RONALD REAGAN, *Ronald Reagan: An American Life*

4. **How have these principles influenced your life decisions and choices?** Please connect each value directly with the resulting decision and please give concrete examples.

_____

_____

_____

_____

_____

_____

_____

_____

_____

_____

_____

_____

_____

_____

_____

_____

_____

_____

_____

_____

**5.** How have these principles defined your life, your family and the person that you are today? Please give examples.

_____

_____

_____

_____

_____

_____

_____

_____

_____

_____

_____

_____

_____

_____

_____

_____

_____

_____

_____

## Today's Tip

Think about the principles that guided your parent's lives. Are yours similar? Or very different? Please describe.

## Quick Quote

"An army of principles can penetrate where an army of soldiers cannot."

— THOMAS PAINE

## Life-Bit

"To say that all people are in principle good would be the same as saying that they are all in principle bad. I would like to respect differences and the uniqueness of each person."

— ROBBERY FRANCIOSI, _Elie Wiesel: Conversations_ _by Elie Wiesel_

"A rich man without charity is a rogue; and perhaps it would be no difficult matter to prove that he is also a fool."

— HENRY FIELDING

"I don't mind helping people I know; friends should depend on each other when the world doesn't treat them well, but no wonder the figures of Charity are made to look so haughty and stuck up in statues."

— MARK TWAIN,
GARY SCHARNHORST,
*Mark Twain:
The Complete Interviews*

6. **What are the top three charities or organizations you have donated to and why?**

_____

_____

_____

_____

_____

_____

_____

_____

_____

_____

_____

_____

_____

_____

_____

_____

_____

_____

_____

_____

_____

## 7. Why do you believe your family should continue that support?
Note: This is your chance to make the case, so please be specific about your thoughts, feelings and the depth of your commitment.

_____

_____

_____

_____

_____

_____

_____

_____

_____

_____

_____

_____

_____

_____

_____

_____

_____

_____

_____

_____

Is there an organization that you always wanted to help but never had the time or resources? If possible, send them even a small sum now or reach out and give them a few hours of your time. If you can't, please write them a letter telling them what you think about their organization.

## Quick Quote

"Deeds of loving-kindness are equal in weight to all the commandments."

— JERUSALEM TALMUD

## Life-Bit

"My father had been 4-F in the war, because of a collapsing lung – despite his repeated and chagrined efforts to enlist. Now – five years after V-J Day – he still went out one night a week as a volunteer to the Civil Air Patrol; he searched the Pittsburgh skies for new enemy bombers."

— ANNIE DILLARD, *An American Childhood*

8. **What are the major volunteer commitments you have made over the years and why did you choose to give your time to them?**

_____

_____

_____

_____

_____

_____

_____

_____

_____

_____

_____

_____

_____

_____

_____

_____

**Just remembered something else?**
**Feel free to use your extra pages at the end of this chapter.**

**9.** **As you have devoted your time and efforts to the things you passionately believe in, why should your family continue to work for those causes?** Please list the most compelling reasons to carry on this work.

_____

_____

_____

_____

_____

_____

_____

_____

_____

_____

_____

_____

_____

_____

_____

_____

_____

_____

**Today's Tip**

Talk to your family about the causes you are most passionate about – even if you think they already know about them.

**Quick Quote**

"There are still many causes worth sacrificing for, so much history yet to be made."

— MICHELLE OBAMA

**Life-Bit**

"At the end of each performance, I made an appeal to the public for help to find some way of giving to others, from my own life, the discovery I had made, and which might liberate and illumine the lives of thousands."

— ISADORA DUNCAN, _My Life_

Did either your mother
or father warn you about
making certain "mistakes"?
What were they? Did you
avoid them or not?

## Quick Quote

"A man's errors are his
portals of discovery."

— JAMES JOYCE

## Life-Bit

"We pass too many of these
marvelous side canyons, to
my everlasting regret, for
most of them will never
again be wholly accessible to
human eyes or feet."

— EDWARD ABBEY,
*Desert Solitaire:
A Season in the Wilderness*

10. **What is the one mistake you made in your life that you would like to save your loved ones from making?** Please be as honest and detailed as possible.

_____

_____

_____

_____

_____

_____

_____

_____

_____

_____

_____

_____

_____

_____

_____

_____

_____

## 11. What is the one decision you made in your life that you are most proud of? Please give some background and tell us why you are proud of it.

_____

_____

_____

_____

_____

_____

_____

_____

_____

_____

_____

_____

_____

_____

_____

_____

_____

_____

### Today's Tip

If possible, call up or write to the person who helped you make a big life decision and relive the process of making that decision. If not, write down what you would have liked to have told them.

### Quick Quote

"In any moment of decision, the best thing you can do is the right thing, the next best thing is the wrong thing, and the worst thing you can do is nothing."

— THEODORE ROOSEVELT

### Life-Bit

"I accept life as it is, the ugliness, the inadequacies, the ironies, for the sake of joy, for the sake of life. It is a comedy. It is slightly ridiculous and full of homeliness. The homeliness my father repudiated at the cost of naturalness. Today I laughed."

— ANAÏS NIN,
_The Diary Of Anaïs Nin: 1931-1934, Volume 1_

Think about a famous person whom you most admire. What is it about their character that makes you look up to them?

## Quick Quote

"I've learned that people will forget what you said, people will forget what you did, but people will never forget how you made them feel."

— MAYA ANGELOU

## Life-Bit

"Despite the disappointment, however, I determined that I would learn something, anyway. I applied myself with greater earnestness than even to the mastering of what was in the 'blue-black' speller."

— BOOKER T. WASHINGTON, *Up From Slavery: An Autobiography*

**12.** **If there's one thing you want your family to understand about you and the choices you've made, what would it be?**
Here's your opportunity to create a lasting understanding, one that will be taken into the future, so feel free to take the time and space as needed to provide as much detail and explanation as you can.

_____

_____

_____

_____

_____

_____

_____

_____

_____

_____

_____

_____

_____

_____

## Don't Forget to PLET!

**Now return to Chapter 2 to add Pivotal Life Events you remembered during this chapter. You'll be glad you did!!**

# 25 Pass-It-On: My Ethical Will

This document will preserve the core values that you identified in Chapter 24 as well as transmit your philanthropic values and history to inspire future generations and encourage them to carry those commitments and contributions forward. This Ethical Will, though not a legal document, is designed for filing with your family lawyer alongside your will and health care proxy. [*Note: Please use your answers to the questions in Chapter 24 to help you fill out this document.*]

The core principles I stand for are _____

_____

_____

_____

My strongest beliefs are _____.

_____

_____

_____

The most powerful influences that shaped my principles and beliefs were _____.

_____

_____

_____

The most important charities/organizations that I have donated to have been _____.

_____

_____

_____

I want my family to continue that support because _____.

_____

_____

_____

My major volunteer commitments have been _____.

_____

_____

_____

I chose to give my time and effort to them because _____.

_____

_____

_____

What I want my family and loved ones to understand about me is _____.

_____

_____

_____

I hope I leave my family, community, country and world better than I found them
because of my _____.

_____

_____

_____

What I hope and pray my descendants accomplish is _____.

_____

_____

_____

The greatest blessing I want to bestow on my family is _____.

_____

_____

_____

# My Memories, Their Legacy: The Greatest Gift

As our LifeJourney adventure draws to a close, we hope you enjoyed each step along the way and that you were able to rise to our challenge to explore the outer borders of your memory and begin to view your own life experiences in brand new ways. We also hope you were able to focus your inner eye on seeing your life as a journey of both body and soul.

As you look back on this LifeJourney experience, please do take this opportunity to pat yourself on the back for a job well done.

We thank you for allowing us to accompany you on this wonderful journey of self-discovery. It has truly been our privilege to be invited into the experiences, feelings and insights that make up your unique life story.

As your LifeJourney coaches, we are confident that, like so many of the participants in our LifeStorytelling "Boot Camps" around the country and around the world, you are now able to recall – and understand - so much more of your life story than you ever thought possible. And we celebrate with you a deepened appreciation of your self and your life story.

Please make one final visit to your PLET (Pivotal Life Events Timeline) which should be quite full by now. You'll want to review it closely to make sure all the moments you can now see as Pivotal Life Events are duly noted there.

And, now that your memory "muscles" are well warmed up, we think you'll enjoy our LifeJourney Books "Just the Facts: My Life in Lists" which you will find in Appendix 1. Your family will thank you for completing the "Where is It?" Check-list in Appendix 2. You will find Appendix 3 to be packed with resources you'll find helpful in tracing your family history. And those of you who are inspired to keep the memoir writing process going will want to read over the Tips and Guidelines we've rounded up for you in Appendix 4.

Those of us here at LifeJourney Books congratulate you. Remember, what your grandmother couldn't do for you, you have now done for your children, grandchildren and your other loved ones. Not only have you performed a wonderful service for future generations who will someday long to know where they came from, but you've discovered your true self in the process. Your grandmother would be proud!

*Deborah Fineblum & Naomi Grossman*

# Appendix 1: Just the Facts: My Life in Lists (and Some of My Favorite Things)

Sometimes we need to sit back and take stock of a life well lived. And making lists can be one of the easiest and most enjoyable ways to do just that. So sharpen your pencil and let's begin!

1. Spouse(s)

2. Children

3. Grandchildren

4. Great-grandchildren

5. Addresses Where I've lived

Addresses          Dates I Lived There

## 6.  Schools I've Attended

Name of School     Town or City     Dates Attended

## 7.  Jobs I've Held

Employer or Company name          Location          Position Held          Dates I Worked
There

## 8.  Best friends

Friends          Approximate Dates of Friendship

## 9.  Childhood hero or heroine

Name          Relationship (if any)

## 10.  Favorite Holiday

## 11.  Favorite Books

Title     Author     Approximate Year Read

## 12. Favorite Songs

Title        Artist     Approximate Year First Heard

## 13. Favorite Movies

Title    Approximate Year Seen

## 14. Favorite Plays

Title        Author        Approximate Year Seen or Read

## 15. Favorite Color

## 16. Favorite Musician

Name        Type of Musician      Approximate Year First Heard

## 17. Favorite Composer

Name        Type of Music     Approximate Year First Heard

## 18. Favorite Artist

| Name | Type of Art | Approximate Year First Seen |
| --- | --- | --- |

# Appendix 2: Where to Find it: What My Loved Ones Need to Know

Whether it's the key to your safe deposit box, your family Bible, your will, account and policy numbers, the deed to the house, the location of priceless family photos or the cemetery (and plot numbers) where your parents and grandparents are buried, knowing that loved ones can locate everything they will need will be a comfort for everyone involved.

## Lawyer

Name:

Name of firm:

Address:

Email:

Phone number(s):

## Investment Company/Broker

Name:

Name of firm:

Address:

Email:

Phone number(s):

## Financial Advisor

Name:

Name of firm:

Address:

Email:

Phone number(s):

## INSURANCE POLICIES

### Health Insurance (including Primary Coverage, Medicare, Medicaid, Medigap, Long-Term Care etc.)

Company:

Policy/account number:


Company:

Policy/account number:


Company:

Policy/account number:


### Life Insurance

Company:

Policy number:

Face amount:

Owner and Beneficiaries


Company:

Policy number:

Face amount:

Owner and Beneficiaries


Company:

Policy number:

Owner and Beneficiaries


### Property Insurance Company:

Policy number:

Brief Description of Property Covered - attach assessor's report

## Home, Real Estate (or Renter's) Insurance

Address of Property

Company:

Policy number:


Address of Property:

Company:

Policy


## Auto Insurance

Company:

Policy


Company:

Policy:


## Any other property that's insured

Company:

Policy/account number:


## OFFICIAL DOCUMENTS

Where is…


**My Will:**


**My Ethical Will (See chapter 25):**


**My Healthcare Proxy Form:**


**My (Durable) Power of Attorney Form:**


## MY ASSETS

**Deed to property (my home and any other real estate)**

Location:

## BANK ACCOUNTS

**Checking:**

Bank or Credit Bureau (and location of bank):

Account number(s):


**Savings:**

Bank or Credit Bureau:

Account number(s):


**Certificates of Deposit (CDs)**

Bank or Credit Bureau:

Account number(s)


## OTHER INVESTMENTS

Name of Broker

Contact Information


**Annuities**

Company:

Policy/Account Number:


Company:

Policy/Account Number:


**Mutual Funds:**

Company:

Policy/Account Number:


Company:

Policy/Account Number:


Company:

Policy/Account Number:

## Money Market Account(s)

Company:

Policy/Account Number:

Company:

Policy/Account Number:

## Stocks

Company:

Policy/Account Number:

Company:

Policy/Account Number:

Company:

Policy/Account Number:

## Bonds

Company:

Policy/Account Number:

Company:

Policy/Account Number:

Company:

Policy/Account Number:

## Safety Deposit Box

Bank or other Institution:

Location:

Account Number:

Key location:

## OUTSTANDING LOANS AND OTHER DEBTS

### Mortgage(s)

Holder: Bank, Credit Union, Mortgage Company, etc.:

Account Number:

### Car Loan

Holder: Bank, Credit Union, Mortgage Company, etc.:

Account Number:

### Other Outstanding Loans

Holder: Bank, Credit Union, Mortgage Company, etc.:

Account Number:

Holder: Bank, Credit Union, Mortgage Company, etc.:

Account Number:

### CEMETERY

Company:

Account Number:

**Outstanding Balance or Paid Off :**

### FUNERAL ARRANGEMENTS

Company:

Account Number:

**Outstanding Balance or Paid Off :**

# FAMILY INFORMATION

**Where the Family Bible and/or Other Family Documents (birth, death, marriage, immigration certificates, etc.) are stored:**

Document:

Location:


Document:

Location:


Document:

Location:


Document:

Location:


**Where Family Photos, Portraits and/or Heirlooms are stored:**

Item:

Location:

Address:


Item:

Location:

Address:


Item:

Location:

Address:


Item:

Location:

Address:

## Where My Parents are Buried

Cemetery:

Location:

Plot:


Cemetery:

Location:

Plot:


## Where My Grandparents are Buried

Cemetery:

Location:

Plot:


Cemetery:

Location:

Plot:


Cemetery:

Location:

Plot:


## Where Other Family Members are Buried

Name:

Relationship:

Cemetery:

Location:

Plot:


Name:

Relationship:

Cemetery:

Location:

Plot:

Name:

Relationship:

Cemetery:

Location:

Plot:


Name:

Relationship:

Cemetery:

Location:

Plot:


## Other Important Items Not Listed Above

Item:

Location:


Item:

Location:


Item:

Location:


Item:

Location:


Item:

Location:

# Appendix 3: Digging Deeper: Your Genealogical Resources

W hy stop at the grandparents? These days, with some clever sleuthing, you can trace your family back farther than you ever dreamed. Here we provide some leading organizations and Web sites to get you started.

The US government has an archives site that offers resources to the amateur genealogist just setting out. It can be accessed here:

http://www.archives.gov/research/genealogy/index.html

It also provides information on access to the U.S. National Archives and Records Administration which can be reached at 1-86-NARA-NARA or 1-866-272-6272

Cyndi's List is another good site as a starting point for researching your family's genealogy. It can be accessed here:

http://www.cyndislist.com/

Note: The site is organized as a categorized and cross-referenced index to genealogical resources on the Internet.

Another good resource for genealogists is Genealogy Resources which has over 70 links to different genealogy resources on the Web. It can be accessed here:

http://www.refdesk.com/factgene.html

If you want to search world archives and are willing to pay a fee, the World Genealogy Archives is a good place to look. It can be accessed here:

http://www.archives.com/genealogy/free-world-genealogy.html

The Website is broken down into countries or regions of the world, making the search relatively simple to use. It provides a free 7-day trial but the last time we checked, a year's access will cost you $40. One note: As the site points out, genealogy records for other countries may not be available in English, so you may have to use translation methods to obtain the information you need.

If you feel you need professional help, hiring a professional genealogist may be the way to go. You can start that search here:

http://www.progenealogists.com/

Good luck!

# Appendix 4:  Continuing Your Memoir – Five Fundamentals for Telling Your LifeStory

"This was the journey he remembered. The actual journey may have been quite different, but the actual journey has no interest for education. The memory was all that mattered." – Henry Adams

**Congratulations, you've completed your *LifeJourney Books Do-It-Yourself Memoir Workbook!***

But that doesn't mean the process of telling your life story has to be over. Now that you've managed to pry open your memory bank, you may be just getting started telling your LifeStories. As you have now experienced, a memory rediscovered begets another and then that one begets another, ad infinitum, especially as you begin to "warm up" your memory muscles and increasingly trust your own recollections.

In fact, the entire process of retrieving, documenting and sharing your life stories can be nothing short of habit-forming.

To give you some guidance on your LifeStorytelling path, here are five LifeJourney tips that will help you continue to build on your memoir:

1.  **Start not at the beginning but in the middle.** For this book, you'll notice we've taken you chronologically through the stages of your life. But if you're embarking on a longer autobiography, feel free to begin at an exciting or life-changing moment. Then back up to the beginning of your life. Or you may wish to begin with your family history. Try rearranging the outline a few times before deciding on the best approach for *your* LifeStory.

2.  **Take your family history up a notch.** If you're like most of us, you know more about one branch of your family tree than the others.  Or one may have some interesting ancestors. Though it's important to do due diligence on every branch and twig that came before, feel free to expand, perhaps devoting an entire chapter to a corner of the family tree you particularly want preserved for posterity.

> *"Where you end up isn't the most important thing.  It's the road you take to get there. The road you take is what you'll look back on and call your life."*
>
> —Tim Wiley

3. **Flesh out part of the skeleton and make it dance.** It might be a difficult time that gave birth to a new strength, insight or appreciation or a moment of greatness, transformation, discovery, drama or historical significance. Write it exactly as it occurred, to the best of your ability. And don't berate yourself for any lapses in memory. As long as you focus on the details – what you saw, smelled, heard and felt, even what you wore – you can't go wrong. And by being honest, not worrying about others will think, you will certainly recall more than you ever thought possible.

4. **Share a day in the life.** If you're writing about a particularly intense chapter of your life, such as in wartime, try recording a typical day, morning to evening. You'll surprise yourself at what these seemingly small daily routines reveal about that time in your life and, as often as not, a particular moment in history as well.

5. **And remember, to thine own self be true.** Shakespeare's words should be the mantra of every memoir writer. When you tell your own experiences and use your own words, not striving after some literary ideal, your true life story will emerge. Tip: Don't be afraid to include snatches of important conversations to the best of your memory, even if you can't recall every word verbatim.

If it's publishing an expanded memoir with photos and documents you're after, you already have the task well begun with your answers to the questions in this workbook. Hopefully, your collection of photos and documents will yield the kinds of treasures you need – indeed, rounding them up often turns out to be an enjoyable family project. And you may find yourself reunited with long-lost family in your quest for photos or details about your family tree.

There are several Web-based services that can help you produce a volume that's both affordable and professional looking, suitable for giving to family, friends and even your town or congregational library. We love Blurb.com but a quick Google search will yield other publishing sites. Please visit us at www.lifejourneybooks.com for additional resources, tips and to learn about the ways we can help you take that next big step in telling your unique life story. While you're there, we hope you take advantage of the opportunity to become part of LifeJourney Books' growing LifeStory Telling family.

# Acknowledgements

The authors want to thank the following individuals who contributed so much to making our *LifeJourney Books Do-It-Yourself Memoir Workbook* a reality:

**Meg Birnbaum** whose magical designs for our cover, logo and graphics continue to delight and inspire us, **Stewart Hirsch** for his pitch-perfect instincts, **Elihu Stone**, Estate Attorney and Insurance Broker extraordinaire for making sure we got the financial advice right, **David Winter**, whose web brilliance and patience continue to be deeply appreciated, **Joe Lucier** for setting us on the path to publication, **our families** for their infinite supply of support and cheer-leading. And last but in many ways most essential: the **LifeJourney Books "Boot Camp" participants**. It is in large part due to their courageous encounters with their own LifeStories that you are able to hold this book in your hands today.

— *Deborah & Naomi*

# About LifeJourney Books

Veteran journalists **Naomi Grossman** and **Deborah Fineblum** started LifeJourney Books to help individuals and groups unearth, document and share their life stories with loved ones while deepening their appreciation of their own unique life journey. *LifeJourney Books Do-It-Yourself Memoir Workbook* grew out of countless memoir-writing "Boot Camps" and coaching sessions Naomi and Deborah have given across the US and Israel.

## Visit Us for All Your LifeStorytelling Needs:

- Memoir-Writing "Boot Camps" and Senior Programs
- LifeStory Coaching
- Interviewing Individuals, Families & Groups
- Multi-media Life Storytelling Opportunities
- Training Staff to Work with Groups in Residential and Day Programs

To schedule the LifeJourney Books program that's right for your senior center or club, retirement community, senior living center or family, or to learn about our training program and *LifeJourney Books Memoir Training Manual*, visit us at www.lifejourneybooks.com, email us at info@lifejourneybooks.com or call LifeJourney Books at (781) 3-MYLIFE (781-369-5433).

While you're exploring our site, you are invited to:

- Sign up for *My LifeJourneys*, the monthly newsletter filled with LifeJourney Books resources and tips for unearthing and preserving your life stories.
- Check out *Senior Moments*, our weekly blog sharing the sometimes funny, other times moving and always inspiring stories from folks around the country and the world who have successfully completed their *Workbook*.
- Add your own favorite LifeStory from your *Workbook*–in 500 words or less. It's easy to do. Just email your excerpt to info@lifejourneybooks.com or send it to LifeJourney Books, 47 Pond Street, Suite 103, Sharon, MA 02067.
- Discover how your senior program, club or living center can take advantage of our *LifeJourney Books Do-It-Yourself Memoir Workbook* group discounts, coaching services and training programs.

*We Look Forward to*

*Taking the Next Steps*

*on Your LifeJourney*

*Together!*

—Deborah & Naomi

www.LifeJourneyBooks.com

20722694R00176

Made in the USA
Charleston, SC
26 July 2013